(3) ed. 1935.

A Dangerous Place

A Dangerous Place

BY

HUGH FLEETWOOD

HAMISH HAMILTON

London

First published in Great Britain 1985
by Hamish Hamilton Ltd
Garden House 57–59 Long Acre London WC2E 9JZ

Copyright © 1985 by Hugh Fleetwood

Map drawn by Patrick Leeson

Poem on page 196 from
FLOWER AND SONG
Poems of the Aztec Peoples
Translated by Edward Kissan and Michael Schmidt
Published by Anvil Press Poetry 1977

British Library Cataloguing in Publication Data

Fleetwood, Hugh
  A dangerous place.
  1. Mexico—Description and travel—1981–
  I. Title
  917.2′04834   F1216.5
  ISBN 0-241-11517-5

Typeset by Rowland Phototypesetting Ltd
Printed in Great Britain by
St Edmundsbury Press, Bury St Edmunds, Suffolk

For

G.M.B.

Contents

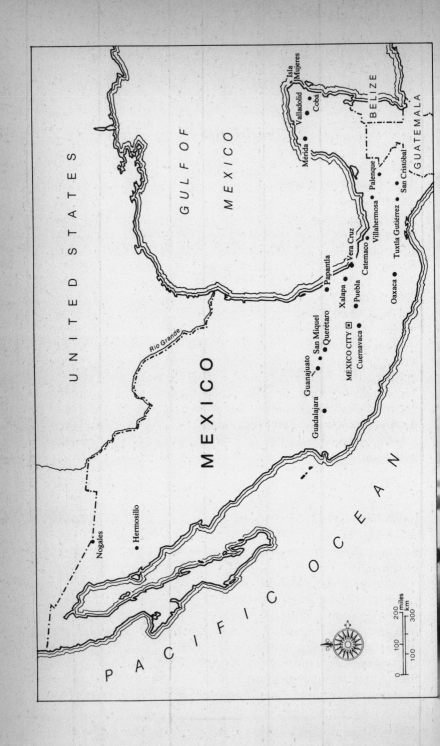

ONE

A Dangerous Place

'You'd better take out insurance, Hugh. Mexico's a dangerous place.'

So my agent had told me eleven days before, when I had gone to say goodbye to him. And so I repeated to myself one Saturday afternoon in January, 1984; as I sat by the window of a Mexicana Boeing, watching the air outside grow steadily greyer as the plane approached Mexico City. Only I changed the still possible 'You'd better take out' to the now impossible 'You should have taken out.'

Mexico's a dangerous place . . .

What was more, I was aware – a certain sense of tightness in my stomach made me aware – my agent's was not an isolated opinion. Mexico has nearly always had a bad press, particularly a bad Anglo-American press; the general view seeming to veer between Graham Greene's absolutely damning 'A country of disappointment and despair', and his cousin Christopher Isherwood's merely smug 'Their ways are not our ways.' But recently, with the collapse of the peso, and Mexico's colossal foreign debt threatening to bring down half the banks of the world, that press had become still worse. And in the months since my publisher had asked me to return to and write a book about a country that I, unlike most others, had – due to some moral failure? – loved when I had been there before, hardly a day had gone by without my reading or hearing some new horror story about my destination.

According to the newspapers, the air in Mexico City was so polluted one could catch hepatitis merely by breathing, the crime rate was so out of control that thieves threw live and hungry rats into your car as you waited at traffic lights – thereby causing you to leap out and lose any valuables you had with you – and corruption was so rife that the former Chief of Police had just fled the country; taking with him a minimum of eleven million dollars in stolen or extorted money, and leaving behind him reports of torture and murder, along with mansions by the sea to which he had flown up to three hundred guests at a time in state-owned helicopters. According to a retired Mexican diplomat now living in England with his wife – a diplomat who gave me letters of introduction to the poet and novelist Octavio Paz, and various other Mexican notables: 'The country's in an impossible situation. If the economists don't tighten the belt, or keep the belt tightened, the whole place is going to fall apart. But if they do tighten it any more or even keep it as tight as it is, as soon as it really starts to hurt the middle classes – as it's beginning to now – there will be social unrest. If there's social unrest the United States will intervene. And if that happens – all hell will break loose.' And a Mexican teacher, whom I had met four years earlier, sent me a letter saying that while he had found me somewhere to live – 'a couple from the Bellas Artes here have got a room you can rent' – and would 'in these days of difficulty and unemployment' have no trouble in finding me a guide and interpreter should I want one, he hoped I wouldn't be too disappointed when I returned, 'because Mexico's changed a lot recently, and isn't what it was.' (I had written to him – having suddenly received a Christmas card after four years of silence – asking, among other things, about the possibility of his finding me a guide, with the excuse that 'absurd though it is for someone who's supposed to be writing some kind of travel book, not only am I not too keen on travelling, but I hate travelling by myself.')

Then a television cameraman, whom I sat next to on a train from New York to Philadelphia (where I stopped off for a few days on my way south, in order to see the friend I had stayed with when I had been in Mexico before) said, when I told him what my ultimate destination was, 'You're going to *Mexico*? Jesus, I was there six months ago. Boy, is that where you see the difference between the First and the Third World. Cripples, beggars – it was like something out of the movies. Well I hope you have a good time, but I must say I don't envy you.' Thus not only fuelling my apprehension, but also reminding me of what, thanks to Hollywood films and most books, I had expected to find when I had first gone there. And had been so certain I would find that I had told Enrique, the friend now living in Philadelphia, that if he wasn't at the airport to meet me when I landed – an airport, I imagined, that would consist of one overgrown runway and one shabby hut lit by a naked lightbulb, where fat and ugly customs officials picked their gold teeth, beat dogs, and threatened to jail one if one didn't slip them a few notes – I would turn round, go straight back to New York, and forget about his country. A country, I further imagined, that was peopled by alcoholic and persecuted priests, overweight and unhappy whores, and moustachioed policemen – the brothers of the customs officials – who, when they weren't persecuting the priests and frequenting the whores, were mutilating revolutionaries and generally doing the dirty work of the few fabulously wealthy individuals who ran and owned the place, and spent most of their time going to parties with Merle Oberon in Acapulco.

And finally, Enrique in Philadelphia, after he had said that this time too he would get someone to meet me at the airport when I arrived (muttering, darkly: 'I wouldn't want anything to happen to you the minute you get off the plane'), told me the story of what had happened to him on his last visit home.

'I was almost kidnapped; walking along the street in broad daylight. I was pushed into a car and had a knife held at my throat. Luckily I lost a shoe in the fight and asked if I could put it on again. When they said yes I smashed the man who was holding the knife in the face with it, grabbed the knife from him, and told the driver of the car I would stab him if he didn't stop. He did, and I jumped out and ran down the street still holding the knife. You should have seen people's faces. But I tell you – I was shaking for two days after.'

Given such a chorus of gloom, it was hardly surprising, as I sat on that aircraft surrounded by mostly elderly, mostly cheerful Americans on their way to the sea, if I did repeat what my agent had told me. Particularly as I wasn't sure what I was going to do when I arrived – never, with one or two exceptions, having liked travel books any more than I have liked travelling, and therefore uncertain whether I would be able to write one myself – and not even sure – my most immediate concern – if anyone *would* be at the airport to meet me. Because Enrique hadn't been able to find his parents on the 'phone before I left – though he had said he would try again – and didn't know how to get in touch with the only other person he knew who might have been free and had a car. A friend who hadn't liked me any more than I had liked her when we had met on my previous trip, and who – though I had thought, back in London, that I might look her up anyway, as I knew almost no one else in Mexico City now – would probably have said no if it had been possible to get in touch.

And not even the knowledge that when I had arrived four years ago, far from finding a one-room shack with customs men I had to bribe, I had found a huge, immaculate, and brand new airport staffed by courteous officials, made me feel in any way more confident.

After all, I told myself – as the plane lurched, the 'Fasten seat belt' sign came on, and I grabbed my arm-rest – hadn't I been told that Mexico had changed?

TWO

Other Voices

Along with my conviction, so similar to that of the television cameraman on the train, that Mexico was a depressing, fly-blown dump, and that the mostly oil-based fabulous wealth that the country nevertheless possessed was in the hands of the fabulously wealthy few, I had believed, before I went there in 1980, that my host's parents, since I knew they weren't among the dirt poor, must be among that tiny group of unimaginably rich.

I would be putting my soul in danger by staying with them, I thought; since here of all places very rich must mean very wicked. But I supposed that for a month or two my soul would be able to stand the strain.

I began to suspect that things were not as I had imagined them almost as soon as I arrived. For as well as seeing that the airport was a clean modern decently-staffed place very much like all large international airports, only pleasanter than most, I saw, when I went with Enrique to pick up his car, that not only were all the other cars in the multi-level car-park what looked to me like quite ordinary cars – Chevrolets, Dodges, Volkswagens, Renaults; the sort of cars that belonged to quite ordinary people, and not to any mythically wicked class – but that Enrique's car itself was of this type. A several-year-old, slightly-battered red Dodge.

Maybe, I thought, he doesn't want to intimidate me.

And my suspicion grew as we drove out of the airport, at six o'clock in the morning. When I saw that not only was the airport similar to other airports, but that the city itself, far from being the open sewer with huts by the side of it that I'd been led to expect, was, with perhaps one great exception, similar, at least in this part of town, to many other big cities. The one great exception being that it struck me, as I looked out of the car at the few people already awake and on the streets, and at the drivers of the other cars on the road, that this was an Indian city. If what I'm looking at is typical of the place as a whole, I told myself, then the middle-classes hold sway here as well; even if, from the look of it, they are middle-classes who aren't yet very secure in their position of power.

Secure or not, if the dominant class did seem to be the middle, then it was quite possible that Enrique himself, whom I didn't know well, and his family . . .

Nevertheless, for all my suspicions, I couldn't help letting my face drop (or so I was told later) when, having turned down a narrow street of closely built white apartment buildings and houses, we pulled up outside a vine-covered wall, and stopped.

'Here,' Enrique said. 'We're home.'

I put my expression down to tiredness, since thanks to snow in New York, and a six hour delay in leaving, I had been awake all night. (As had Enrique who, half-believing my threat to turn round and leave if I wasn't met at the airport, had been waiting there since midnight.) But, though I didn't confess it, it was not tiredness at all that caused the drop. It was disappointment. I had been expecting some vast villa with gold taps and servants and swimming pools. I had been expecting depravity. I had been *hoping* for depravity.

Instead of which . . .

Disgusted with myself, I tried – clearly not successfully – to smile.

'Well,' I said, 'it's good to be here.'

We let ourselves in, through a gate in the vine-covered wall, to a small well-watered garden with an African tulip tree growing in the middle of it. We opened the front door of a small two-storey house with a Christmas tree in one corner of its blue-carpeted living room. And we went upstairs where I was shown to the guest room and where I told myself, as I got into bed and fell asleep, 'You cur.'

No wonder I have always believed that writers, and artists in general, are the creatures of the powerful.

A feeling of guilt for my initial reaction never entirely left me, all the time I was in Mexico in 1980. Either because my disappointment itself, though it kept well out of sight after the morning of my arrival, never quite left me, or, as I prefer to think, because throughout my stay I was treated with such kindness by my hosts that I could never forget with what thoughts I had come into their house. And while it never managed to wake the other larger guilt that I felt was sleeping inside me – the guilt for loving a country that had so many obvious warts, and had always been so condemned by others – it always threatened to; and thus made it difficult for me ever, entirely, to relax.

What would happen if the beast did awake, I wondered.

It might become impossible to ignore.

*

I was reminded of this first arrival of mine, and of my subsequent feelings of guilt, when, four years later, I once again got off a plane in Mexico City. Got off to find – of course – that I was neither mugged as I came down the aircraft steps, nor that the airport was any less clean, modern and efficient than it had been before. It was seeing someone waving at me as I passed through immigration, and realizing that Enrique must have managed to get in touch with his parents, that brought it back to me. That – and the idea that passed through my mind that I should, perhaps, once again feel guilty; for having obliged an elderly couple, one of whom had recently had a heart attack, to trek across a city of seventeen million people in order to pick me up.

I decided not to only when Mrs F kissed me and said 'Oh Hugh we are so glad to see you, but you must be careful. Mexico is very changed now, and is very dangerous.'

However, if four years ago I had been struck, once we had left the airport, by how similar Mexico City was to most other big cities, this time, after we had picked up the car and had started our drive towards the apartment where I was, with luck, expected, I was struck by something – at any rate in part – different. Initially – and though I had noted this before, I had somehow forgotten it – by how very much the population of Mexico City is Indian; for all that one expects it to be as vaguely Iberian-looking as the one- or two-storey colonial houses that still survive amidst the shabby modern high-rises. Not, in most cases, totally Indian. Not, in a few cases, Indian at all. But in general, and as a first impression – yes, Indian. (And for some reason – perhaps because one is led to believe otherwise by those Hollywood films, and by those Anglo-American novels, even if one has been here before and knows it to be true, the fact is, or remains, surprising. This is an Indian city, one tells oneself; and not, despite the sense of a dominant middle class, and the fact that that dominant middle class tends more towards the white than the brown, a city of principally European descent. An *Indian* city.

Or perhaps it is because in this respect one imagines Mexico to be like its neighbour to the north; that either destroyed, engulfed, or confined its past to a reservation. Discovering that here the past lives on, one cannot help but be taken slightly aback. How strange, one tells oneself: here there has been no real break.

Maybe that's why the country's in the state it's in . . .)

But the other, and perhaps more surprising thing that struck me as we made our way across town, was that far from conditions, as I'd been told, having changed for the worse in my absence, they seemed, as far as one can judge such matters from a car, if anything to have improved. The sky, though murky from the air, from here on the ground appeared clear and bright and blue. The people going about their business in the streets and in the shops looked, on the whole, cheerful and better-dressed than I remembered. And – though this didn't stop me from keeping mine closed – if the evidence of open car windows was anything to go on, nobody apart from me had even heard about flying rats, let alone was worried about them if he or she had.

Social unrest? A dangerous place? Well maybe, I thought – as Mr F, with an indifference as grand as it was alarming, drove the wrong way down a one-way street in which he neither noticed what he was doing, nor saw the waves, more startled than angry, of the policemen who, from their parked car, tried to flag him down. But for the moment – I reserved my judgement.

And in fact, after that one final statement of the gloom motif by Mrs F at the airport, this note of reassurance was one I was to hear repeated often, by almost everyone and everything, that first day back in Mexico. (And not only that first day: for some time after my arrival I was to hear it, ringing out clearly in contrast with the former dirge.)

To begin with, though I had worried that the couple who were going to put me up had not received the letter telling them of my arrival, I need not have. For after we had driven down a quiet leafy street lined almost exclusively by colonial houses – all pink and white and red and green, with wrought-iron work on the balconies and windows, and rubber trees in their gardens – we pulled up outside one of the few modern buildings. And when I got out of the car, rang a bell, and had the street door opened for me by a slim dark-haired young woman who introduced herself as Sonia, I was told that of course they had received it – 'Almost a week ago.'

Just as one knows that the Mexicans are all vaguely Iberian looking, so one knows that the Mexican postal system is unreliable . . .

Then 'Oh things aren't *that* bad,' José – the other half of the couple – told me, when, having said goodbye to the F's, and having been shown up to a small apartment on the fourth floor, I mentioned that I had read a report which stated that the air was liable to ignite spontaneously here one day, and consume whole areas of the city in a gigantic fireball. 'In fact,' he said, pointing out of the window towards the snow-covered mountains which were, somewhat hazily, visible in the distance, 'they've finally started doing something about the pollution. Not much. But it's a start.'

'Yes,' I told him. 'Four years ago I think I saw the mountains just twice in two months.'

And finally Gerardo, the teacher who had sent me the Christmas card, and who had found me this place, turned up and added his voice to the now more reassuring chorus. It is true that he said that he too had been to the airport but had clearly missed me; and when I apologized and told him he shouldn't have bothered, added 'Oh that's all right, too many's better than too few, and nowadays it's better to be on the safe side.' As it is true that both he and José, once we had settled down to have a drink, told me 'Yes of course the police here are corrupt'; before going on to give me accounts of friends who had had necklaces and bracelets taken off them when stopped for so-called traffic violations, who had risked rape when pulled over to the side of the road on the pretext of having their documents checked, and had been obliged to pay bribes. But even he felt compelled to conclude his welcoming speech on the up-beat rather than the down. 'Still,' he said, 'things seem to be starting to improve. I mean at least the cops aren't allowed to cruise round by themselves now. So with any luck, if you don't have to bribe the lot of them – there's *some* measure of protection.'

Indeed, so very much did the pendulum seem to have swung the other way, that by the time night fell I was almost prepared to dismiss everything I had heard before as, if not nonsense, at any rate exaggeration. I still told myself that I reserved my judgement, and I was aware that even if the picture I was now presented with was less threatening than the one I had had thrust under my nose hitherto, it wasn't another picture altogether. Nevertheless, as I sat in that small comfortable apartment, with its Miró and Picasso lithographs, with its palms and its ferns and its Chinese ivory carvings, with its mirrors and its great window that constituted one entire wall of the living room – and as I listened to José talking about his stereo, and his holidays, and how of course it was perfectly safe to go out here after dark, even for Sonia – I almost instinctively found myself repeating what I had told myself earlier in the car. A dangerous place, indeed.

Yet though I was reassured by all I was told and saw that day – and thought that José and Gerardo were probably more accurate witnesses than any foreign correspondent or expatriate Mexican – it wasn't till I went out for a walk that evening, to take a look at the neighbourhood, that I felt I had heard the final word – for the time being – on Mexico and its dangers. The final word and also, possibly, the true voice of Mexico itself. It came to me, this voice, in the smell of tropical vegetation that, even on this comparatively chilly night, seemed to wrap itself around one like a thick soft blanket; a blanket reeking of ripeness, quick growth, and easy rottenness. And the message it whispered as I walked along and tried to think where and how I should start the portrait I had come here to paint, now that my canvas had been, so to speak, prepared, was 'Relax. Relax. After all – what does it matter what happens? What does anything matter . . .'

Even if it were a false voice, it would be difficult, I suspected, not to heed it.

THREE

The Background

Around thirty thousand years ago nomadic tribes from Central Asia crossed the Bering Straits and moved slowly south. On the great plains they would remain nomadic, but when they reached "Mesoamerica" – and when the animals they hunted became extinct – they started to settle. In order to grow and store the crops and vegetables they now became dependent on, they had to form themselves into societies, make astronomical calculations to determine when best to plant those crops, produce pottery and develop a common language. And in order to control their societies and protect their fields from attack, they had to organize politically. With political organization there emerged, inevitably, a "ruling class", a class composed of either those responsible for the protection of the fields, or those who maintained what was most essential in this part of the world: the irrigation system. With a ruling class there also emerged three other groups, whose duty it was to support the community and maintain the position of those in power: the military, the priests, and the artists. And with the emergence of both masters and servants, culture began to develop into civilization . . .

The first such civilization to leave a clear record of itself in Mesoamerica was that created, from about 2000 B.C. onwards, by those Indians who were known, if only afterwards and by others, as the Olmecs. They settled round the southern part of the Gulf of Mexico; and their influence on all subsequent civilizations was profound . . .

"Olmec," in Nahautl (the language of the Aztecs among others) means "Men of the rubber forests."

So, the morning after my arrival, I learned, as I went through the Anthropological Museum in Mexico City. The museum that is the first stop in Mexico City most visitors make, the museum that had been the first stop I had made four years ago, and the museum that Gerardo had suggested last night should again be my first stop this time. Not only to help me find my feet, and acclimatize myself, but also to give me a background against which I could work. An idea I had thought a good one. But as I wandered round, feeling indeed quite relaxed now, and as I talked to Gerardo – who had also told me last night that he was on vacation at the moment, and until classes started again at the university where he taught he himself was prepared to act as my guide and interpreter – I noticed something I hadn't noticed on my previous visit. Something that made me think that while this museum might not provide me with the background I had thought it would – that, simply, of the history of Mexico – it might, instead, provide me with another. A background, what was more, that was of greater interest than the one I had thought to find. And the further round the museum I went, and the longer I looked at the sculptures and statues on display, the more I felt certain that what I had noticed was not just a passing impression.

What I noticed was this. That though the Olmecs, those first settlers of whom we have any record, had – through trade and to a certain extent through warfare – a great influence on all subsequent Mesoamerican cultures, they alone displayed any trace of idealism in their art; and, more particularly, in their representation of man.

The later cultures – the Maya of Guatemala and the Yucatan peninsula, the Téotihuacans from just north of present day Mexico City, the Toltecs based in Tula who both destroyed the Olmecs (as they did, later, the Maya) and diffused their culture, the Zapotecans of Oaxaca, and all the other tribes up to and including the Aztecs – sculpted humans and animals either realistically, or in a stylized fashion; with their realism heightened by simplification. (And to eyes trained in any European tradition these faces and figures are not beautiful. Both because aesthetically they are outside the European tradition, and because they do simply represent man as he is.)

The Olmecs, however, while also portraying men and women who do not correspond to European ideas of beauty, did so – in a number of cases, if not in all – not by trying to reproduce those men and women exactly as they were, but by trying to reproduce the idea that the sculptor had of them. In other words, their sculptors tried to produce an image, or even a dream, rather than the thing itself. And insofar as they succeeded, they gave their finished work a more universal appeal, a sense of reality, that no merely realistic reproduction could ever have had. If only because no work of the imagination, no dream, however unusual or bizarre, is outside any tradition, or seems entirely unreal.

Moreover, by trying to reproduce the ideas of their subjects, rather than the subjects themselves, the Olmec sculptors introduced an element of the what-should-be into their work, rather than the what, simply, is. For their vision was affected by how they looked at their subjects, what they thought of their subjects, and what they – and thus to a certain extent the society in which they lived – thought of all men and women.

Because there is this element of idealism in Olmec culture, certain Olmec sculptures are more readily accepted and appreciated by the European eye accustomed to European standards of beauty than are, for example, more decorative and baroque works by Maya sculptors, magnificent though some of these may be. But further, I told myself as I returned and returned again to the Olmec room, this trace of idealism in Olmec culture – and the lack of it in all subsequent cultures – must go some way towards explaining the following four thousand years of Mexican history. Towards explaining why the Olmecs became both the first of all Mesoamerican tribes to create a civilization, and the tribe that would influence all others. Towards explaining why, as the Olmecs' influence was replaced by that of the Téotihuacans, as the Toltecs went south to conquer the Maya, and as the Aztecs moved in from the north, settled in Tenochtitlán (Mexico City) and subdued most of their neighbours, while all these different societies created their own cultures and made their own contribution to Mesoamerican civilization as a whole, that civilization did not really develop very much, and certainly not as much as the civilization of Europe was developing at the same time. (How could it, when there was no dream of what a man should be to pursue?) And towards explaining why, when the Spanish invaded in 1519, the Aztecs, and most of the other Indians – even granted the Spaniards' possession of guns and horses – were so quickly overcome.

For whether their idealism was the father of their greed for gold, or their greed for gold the father of their idealism, idealistic the Spanish – and all the European colonizers – were; at least when they first arrived. They had a very distinct vision – a dream

– of what a man should be; and an almost equal consciousness of how far they fell short of attaining that dream.

A consciousness that was at the root of their dissatisfaction with their own lands; and their longing for some metal that would dazzle their eyes, and prevent them from seeing their failings.

The reason why the Olmecs had that trace of idealism in their culture will probably always remain a mystery; just as the reason why any culture has it or had it will probably always remain a mystery. But that they did have it I became, as I went round the Anthropological Museum, convinced.

One only had to look.

Confident that I had now been given a background against which I could work – and been given, as a result, the desire to get out and start working – I came to feel that my process of settling in, that had started yesterday afternoon, was complete. I'm going to be all right, I thought, as Gerardo and I decided we had had enough culture for one day. And Mexico's going to be all right. And from now on I'll have no more doubts about my presence here, and what I'm going to do here. To hell with any fears. And to hell with any preconceived ideas as to what a travel book, a true book, should be about.

For a start, I told my companion as we headed for the exit, I was not going to use the letters of introduction I'd been given; since they were all to, in one capacity or another, 'official' people; and if I did use them I would end up with an official version of the truth; with an official portrait of Mexico.

'Which I don't want.'

Secondly, I went on – as we started walking across the park in which the museum stands – I was not going to go to the opposite extreme, and start, literally, slumming it. Both because it seems to me wrong to use suffering, however minimally, as entertainment, and because anyone who wants to know what life is like in the lower depths knows already: from newspapers, magazines, and television documentaries.

'The garbage-strewn streets. The carcasses of dogs. The rats, the dust, the pigs nosing around in the mud outside and inside shacks that have no sanitation, whose walls are made at best of corrugated iron and at worst of cardboard. The children whose noses are perpetually running, whose eyes are perpetually red, and who perpetually suffer from bronchial or intestinal complaints; brought on by the dampness, the dirt, and the fact that even the so-called drinking water – which may come from a single tap a mile away – is so contaminated it has live insects in it. Out of two and a half million children born in Mexico in 1980 one and a half were suffering from physical or mental handicaps caused by malnutrition, and one third will die before they are six. Most of the children – and most of the inhabitants of the slums are children – don't know how old they are, and not having a birth certificate sometimes can't go to school; or not until they have lost a year or two, trying to prove that they exist. And when, around the age of fourteen or fifteen, they stop being children and start having children, if the men can get a job they tend to drink the money away; to forget the rats, and the dust, and the pigs nosing around . . .'

There is a danger, I said, that if one does go round saying, or describing, how terrible it is to be poor – instead of trying to discover, or show, the ultimate reasons for that poverty – one will end up envying the unhappy their unhappiness.

'And that, in my opinion, is worse than envying the happy their happiness.'

And third, I said, as we went into a restaurant to have lunch, just because I believed I had made a discovery this morning, I was not going to spend the next however many months mining one exclusive seam. Nor trying to force my picture into some already-made frame. No, I was just going to lead as normal a life – in Mexico – as possible, doing what I liked doing and meeting who I met, and to hope that, at the end, my subject would look natural against the background I had given it. Or the background I'd been given.

'Mexico: An unofficial portrait.'

I spent the rest of that day, after we had eaten, wandering round the grey overcast city and talking with Gerard. We discussed the desire of most young Mexicans either to go north to the States or across to Europe, and the fact that one could always tell if babies were of Indian descent here because when they were born, and for the first five months of their lives, they had a dark patch at the base of the spine. ('You'll be telling me they have tails, next!') And we talked of my idea, and the impression that my first visit had given me, that dark patches or no, Mexico was predominantly an Indian country. An Indian country, it went without saying, that had been enormously influenced by its contact with Europe – and particularly with a Spain that had, I suggested, started to suffer its own crisis of idealism soon after the invasion – and had been and would be greatly influenced by its neighbour to the north; which, even more than Mexico itself, was a child of idealism, and had yet to suffer any real crisis of that idealism. Nevertheless, for all the scorn cast upon the idea by many Mexicans, still, to a great degree, Indian.

'And I don't just mean racially.'

And then, around eight o'clock, having agreed to set off on a trip south of the city the day after – by way of renewing my acquaintance with the countryside – we separated; Gerardo going to ask his landlady if we could borrow her car for a few days, and I going home. To read, to go to bed, and, having tried to convince myself that just because there hadn't been a major earthquake for the last four years that didn't necessarily mean there would be one while I was staying here, to sleep.

I made myself think of the Olmecs in the night when I woke and wondered why the window was rattling . . .

But in the morning, when I got up and we left on what Gerardo called 'the second stage of my refresher course,' I was reminded that a lack of idealism wasn't the only element in the background against which any portrait of Mexico must be painted.

FOUR

The Natural World

Another consequence of my idea that Mexico was a seedy ram-shackle place was that I had believed, before I came the first time, that the landscape of Mexico was similarly squalid; the physical equivalent of the moral state.

A blasted defeated wilderness, glared down upon by an un-kind sun.

I had been unprepared, therefore, not just for finding that the country was beautiful – most countries, in their different ways, are beautiful, even the most squalid – but also, and more, for finding that it was softly, generously beautiful; comparable, in my experience, only with Italy at its best. There was, far from unkindness, a gentleness about the light; there was, far from squalor, a sense of richness, ripeness, fullness about the land. And having been unprepared – I was overwhelmed.

'I had,' I told Enrique, 'no idea.'

But over the years, if one doesn't forget what one has seen, one occasionally forgets one's reaction to what one has seen, or pretends it wasn't what it was. And so, over the years, I had forgotten or started pretending; particularly over the last few months. Well, yes, of course it was all right, I had started to tell myself; but I only thought it extraordinary because I was happy there. If I went back . . .

This time I'd see the truth.

With the result that when I did go back, I was almost as unprepared for what I saw a second time as for what I'd seen the first. Or even more unprepared perhaps, having in the interval convinced myself that what was, was not. And being, once again, unprepared, I was, once again, overwhelmed.

To begin with, as, the day after our visit to the museum, Gerardo and I drove as far as we could up Popocatepetl, one of the two great volcanoes overlooking Mexico City, I tried to resist what I told myself firmly was 'this mere appearance of loveliness.'

'You're here,' I went on – as I got out of the car, felt a pain in my chest when I breathed the thin cold air, and twisted my ankle in one of the many volcanic rat burrows that undermine the ash covered mountainside – 'to see something more. What lies behind the mere appearance.'

Ugliness. Misery. Dread.

But then, as I looked across the pine forests and the valleys towards the other great volcano, Iztaccihuatl, and began to feel exhilarated by the altitude, rather than hurt, my defences started to weaken. I mean really, I thought, why . . . ?

And by the time we had driven down to the warmth again, to the small bright town of Amecameca, where the produce in the market was so abundant that it almost made one overlook the neatly pruned trees in the square, the scarlet irises, the church standing up against the white snow-tipped volcano, and the white snow-tipped volcano standing up against the clear blue winter sky, those defences had disappeared completely. Yes, one tells oneself confronted with such beauty, darkness exists. But the inevitability of night in no way diminishes the glory of the sun. Quite the opposite, if anything. And here, where the sun is dazzling . . .

What is more, I continued, if one is going to write about this country, one *must* recognize the fact that Mexico is beautiful. For it is in this setting that the people one is going to be talking to and talking about grew up, and live; and while it may be impossible to say why a particular nation has – or doesn't have – certain plants in its cultural undergrowth, the land in which that undergrowth is rooted must have some bearing on the eventual shape, texture, or indeed existence or non-existence of those plants.

By which I mean that if there is some lack of idealism in the Mexican character, that lack must have something to do with the fact that nature is itself so ideal here that one feels one has no need of dreams; of that which might be, of that which should be. There is no need to long for anything else, when the what-is is so very, so exuberantly splendid.

(Or, I should add at this point, when the what-is is so bleak that no amount of dreaming could do much to improve it. Because up to now, neither on my previous trip nor on this, had I travelled north of Mexico City. Had I done, I might have thought that the stories I had heard about Mexico were true. A blasted, defeated wilderness . . . though my conclusions would not have been different, even so. For one thing because, by and large, the more barren lands to the north had never been Indian country; or when they had been, those Indians had not created a lasting civilization, the Aztecs themselves not developing culturally until they reached the fertile lakelands in the valley of Mexico around the year 1350. And for another, because there the land, in many places, was so inhospitable that even the cactus looked as it were having difficulty taking root. And where cactus is unwelcome, idealism is as unlikely to flourish as it is, perhaps, in a place where anything and everything will grow.)

This renewed, if at the time partially ignorant sense of the magnificence of the Mexican landscape – and the feeling that one would have to be a great puritan not to love it – stayed with me for the next four days. It stayed with me as we drove from Amecameca to Cholula; a town which boasts of having as many churches as there are days in a year, and what had once been the biggest pyramid in Mexico. (Though now, unless one goes into the corridors which run through it, the pyramid appears to be only a church-topped, grass- and tree-covered hill.) It stayed with me as we went from Cholula to Puebla – notable for the tiled façades of its houses, its elaborate wrought-iron work, and its air of being a sedate matron of a town where, if the middle-classes elsewhere are having difficulties, here are doing very nicely indeed thank you – and then made our way back across country to Taxco. And it stayed with me as we drove from Taxco – a small former silver mining town in the mountains that even tourist books dismiss as touristy, but that is, nevertheless, with its steep cobbled streets, its colonial architecture, and its churrigueresque cathedral, pretty – to Cuernavaca. Where we arrived after dark, realized we had forgotten the key to the house on the outskirts of town that belonged to some friends of Gerardo, and had to climb over a wall – with the local dogs snapping at our legs – and remove a pane of glass from the kitchen window, round which the putty was still soft from the last time it had been removed.

'Everybody,' Gerardo explained, as I stood in a midnight-black flower bed, trying to make sure the pane didn't fall out and break, and expecting at any moment to be bitten by something more unpleasant, now, than a dog, 'always forgets their keys when they come here.'

And not even the reminder – once we had climbed unharmed into the house, flicked some switches, and seen that the garden, finally illuminated, had bougainvillaea plunging purple off the walls and roses growing white and yellow round its edges – that nature had another face, could lessen this sense or make me feel anything other than overwhelmed.

That night, as I was making up my bed in a small, chilly, almost unfurnished room, I knocked the corner of the iron bedstead against the white stuccoed wall. It wasn't a hard knock, but as if the plaster had the thinnest of skins, it was hard enough to crack it. And immediately, out of the crack, like blood from beneath that thin skin, poured a river of black ants. A river that ran down the white wall and across the red tiled floor; a river that we only managed, after fifteen minutes, to turn back with boiling water and sprays; and a river that was repulsive not so much for its composition, as for the way it had flooded out so instantly. It made one feel that those ants had been waiting there for years just to be released – and to discover the price of freedom – and that that whole wall was, probably, a living thing; which, if one should even tap it at any other point, might release not only ants, but other creatures far worse. Demons, beasts, and *'horrors without name'*.

And the following morning, after an almost sleepless night – afraid that if I turned over the very air I displaced might cause the plaster to crumble – when I got up to make myself some coffee, on taking a cup down from a sealed cabinet, I found a cockroach sitting in the bottom of it. A cockroach so gigantic that not only did I drop the cup on the floor, but didn't dare get another from the cabinet, in case I found the monster's mate. (And the morning after that, though Gerardo and I spent an hour washing out all the cups and plates in the cabinet, when I again went to make myself some coffee, I did find the monster's mate. Thereafter, though we stayed one more night at the house, using it as a base as we toured the countryside round Cuernavaca, and though I didn't see any other living thing in the house, I gave up the idea of having coffee when I woke: or at any other time.)

No – none of this mattered. Ants, cockroaches, and other reminders of mortality – or whatever – were simply the turning of the earth. They did not obscure the light. And though Cuerna- vaca itself, despite a nearly perfect climate, was, this second time around, just as ugly as I remembered it, by the time Gerardo and I had finished our tour, and were driving back to Mexico City – through a rain-storm that made the forested mountain road treacherous, and caused trucks to slide off the tarmac and me to fear we were about to – I was ready to tell him that if one came here determined not to see beauty, then one might just as well not come at all.

'And,' I added, as our windscreen wipers stopped working, making it more likely that we would join the crashed trucks, 'I mean it.'

Because Mexico, I wrote in my diary the following day, 'is, as the holiday brochures say, "the land of flowers". And there is little point in going to a garden without looking at the flowers, whatever else is on show there.'

The land of flowers; and not art, or dreams, or ideals . . .

And that, possibly, is both its glory and its tragedy.

*

Thus prepared, I settled into my room in the city, determined not to move again for a while. I established a routine of newspaper reading, breakfast with José and Sonia, writing, lunch, exploration, people-meeting and, or, entertainment. (Well, newspaper-reading of a sort. The following is fairly typical of Mexico's English language paper, much of which is given over to the doings of the American community in the country: 'Grace Robbins had a delightful party the other night at her home. She looked stunning in a mini black dress and with her long hair it was something. Raul of Raul & Tony fame serenaded us with a few songs, but that was after dinner. Dinner was a complete Mexican dinner with tamales that were outstanding. After everyone had eaten their fill the musicians started up again and that's when everyone asked Raul to sing so he did. We also did a bit of dancing. The best dance of all was the one done by Grace and Raul, how to describe it. The closest I can come is to say it was a swingrumba, really something.')

I did a little more dipping into the history of Mexico, learning about that period between 1519 when Cortes invaded the country, and 1810, when Hidalgo and Allende started the movement for independence from Spain. A period characterized on the one hand by the constant division between the Indians – who in 1800 numbered three and a half million out of a total population of six million – and the Creoles and Mestizos; and on the other by the increasing division between the Creoles and Mestizos – who wanted to run the country – and the Spain-born Spanish, who actually did. And I declined an offer of eating my lunch with my hosts as well; on the grounds that my Spanish wasn't up to having a conversation with them, and that when I was in their company, communication, with Sonia in particular, whom I found more difficult to understand than José, tended to be limited to an occasional, explosive 'Hugh!' accompanied by a good-natured smile (to which I could only reply, with what I hoped was an equally good-natured smile 'Sonia!'), followed by the enquiry 'Como estas?' – 'How are you?'

'Bien, bien,' I always told her.

'Bien?' said Sonia, looking relieved. 'Ah,' she would then sigh, shaking her head and returning to her food: 'Que bien.'

On the whole, I preferred one of the many little restaurants in the street; where I could eat a set meal for a dollar, and read . . .

And then, deciding that a concert was the best way of attacking what I had come to think of as my canvas, I set off; so relaxed by now I could hardly believe that I had ever felt doubtful about coming here.

'It's extraordinary how quickly one changes!'

It was only when I had set off that I began to think that what my agent had told me was, after all, true.

Mexico is a dangerous place.

FIVE

A Mexico City Diary

Monday, February 6

For as long as I have liked music, or maybe even longer, I have known the name Victoria de los Angeles. I saw it on record covers as a child; I read it in newspapers when I was growing up; and I heard it on the radio before I really knew who she was. But though when I did start liking music I occasionally bought one of her records, and though when I started going to concerts I often saw that she was singing here or there, for some reason I never actually heard her in person. The nearest I got to it was once in London, when I went so far as to buy a ticket for a recital she was giving. However, while I turned up for the event she, unfortunately, didn't; being sick. Which made me think that she was destined to remain just a name for the rest of my life. One of those names that would never be forgotten, but one of those names that, despite records and the radio, would always remain mythical; like a place one has heard of and seen photographs of but never actually visited. So that not having seen the way the light falls on certain buildings, not having felt the mood of the place, though one is confident one knows it, one cannot be sure that it is as the photographs show it to be. One cannot be sure, in fact, that it is the place one has always imagined it to be.

But yesterday, my first day back in town after my motor trip with Gerardo, I bought the local English language paper, *The News*, saw an advertisement for a 'song recital by Victoria de los Angeles', and realized that at last I had caught up with the singer. And this time, I felt certain, she would not be sick, would not escape me. This time, I thought, I've got her.

And not only will I hear someone whose name I've always known, but I will see Mexico City's *haute bourgeoisie*, and the Palacio de Bellas Artes, at the same time.

If, that is, José, working as he did at the Bellas Artes, could get me a ticket (since he told me that the concert had been sold out for days), and if, at the age Victoria de los Angeles had to be now – because the concert she hadn't shown up for in London had been almost twenty years ago, and she had been performing for at least twenty years before that – anyone at all could hear her.

Maybe I shouldn't go, I tried to persuade myself; so that I wouldn't be too disappointed if I didn't get a ticket. It really isn't fair. It is like trying to tell what a day is like from the quality of the evening. Or like trying to tell what Tenochtitlán was like from the few remaining stones, and the one or two artefacts that the Spanish didn't destroy.

But José did get me a ticket, fair or not of course I went, and despite the years I think I did get a pretty good idea of the day; of the former, lovely city.

First, though, the building.

Started at the turn of the century, the Palacio de Bellas Artes stands at one end of the Alameda Park, a rectangular formal garden, originally used for burning heretics, that constitutes, along with the Zocalo – the Cathedral square – the centre of Mexico City. It is an overblown, pompous, off-white marble building that was designed during the 'Presidency' of Porfirio Díaz. And just as Díaz himself, who was dictator from 1877 to 1911, was the creature and champion of the upper-middle-classes – opening up Mexico to foreign investment and developing industry and commerce, but so neglecting the land and those who worked it that two thirds of that land was in the hands of just over eight hundred people, and the condition of the Indian population was if anything worse than it had been in 1600 – so the Palacio de Bellas Artes almost has to be seen as a monument to those upper-middle-classes. It is heavy; it is ornate; in its way with its Tiffany glass curtain and its style, midway between art nouveau and art deco, it is magnificent (inside, at least); and despite the fact that it is slowly sinking into the former lake-bed on which it is built (twenty feet in fifty years) it has so far not only remained standing, but has continued, along with the Cathedral and a sky-scraper called the Latino-Americano built opposite it, to dominate the city; both architecturally and culturally. How much longer it will continue to do so depends presumably on whether its patrons will be willing sooner or later to spend the cash necessary to stop the great thing disappearing into the slime.

One suspects they will be, but . . . who knows? Maybe by then – in another fifty years or so – they will give a collective sigh of 'Oh well, what the hell, we've had a pretty good run for our money;' and just lie back and wearily, almost contentedly, watch their monument ooze away beneath their feet.

Right then, these patrons: what do they look like, as they take their seats for the concert?

For a start, they are less sleek, less predatory, less menacing than I had imagined them; more lumpy, dumpy, homely. (Like English audiences when they dress up for an occasion, they would look better if they didn't bother. The women, for the most part, seem self-conscious and awkward in their off-the-shoulder dresses, their skirts of uncertain length; and those men who are wearing suits seem simply uncomfortable.) The next thing one notices about them is that they all appear to know each other; there is a continual waving, a toing and froing and blowing of kisses that makes one feel one has wandered into a club to which one doesn't really belong.

A club to which one doesn't really belong; but a club into which one would probably be admitted if one asked to be.

Because one is recognizably middle-class oneself? Because one is there in the first place?

Yes, partly that. But principally – and this is the third thing one notices about the audience, and there is no ignoring the fact in this Indian country – because ninety-five per cent of the people present are white. Sure, they are, most of them, recognizably Mexican; the dark hair, the heavy features, the exuberant women and the, on the whole, rather diffident men. And sure, there is some Indian blood in many, if not all, of them; which accounts, to a large degree, for the heaviness of feature and the stockiness of figure. (The combination of Indian and Iberian is not, one tells oneself – and one will be told often in Mexico – a happy one, physically.) Nevertheless, just as in the streets outside the predominant colour is brown, so inside the predominant colour is white. One knows that if one asks any of these people how they think of themselves, they will say 'Mexican'; by which they will mean both Indian and Spanish. But their way of talking, and everything about them, will not only proclaim that they think of themselves as being primarily of European origin, but that they think of 'the Indians' as being a race apart: a race which, despite a

drop of blood here and there, has nothing to do with them
personally.

However, having said all this, as the lights start to go down,
and one notes that though one had expected the concert to start at
least half an hour late it is in fact just eight thirty-three – a mere
three minutes late – and that, still more surprisingly, everyone
has taken his or her seat, one has to conclude that give or take a
flower or two in the hair, and allowing for the overdone waves,
kisses, and 'Olá como estas?'s, this audience is very much like a
concert anywhere in the world. That is, there are a large number
of businessmen and their wives who would rather be elsewhere;
there are an almost equally large number of slightly earnest
young people; and there are a disproportionate number of what
look like old Austrian Jewish ladies. Where do they all come from
one wonders as one sees them; so neat, so quiet, so sharp-
tongued and melancholy? Did they all manage to leave Austria
before Hitler took over? And how come that there are so many
still living, and that they never seem to die off? Perhaps there is
some country where they still raise them; these exiles who heard
Mengelberg conduct, knew Bruno Walter personally, and can't
help but admire Furtwängler, whatever he did in the war.
Perhaps the music keeps them going. Or perhaps the explanation
is another. That if one goes to enough concerts during one's
life, especially concerts of the Viennese masters, eventually,
around the age of seventy, one turns into an old Austrian Jewish
lady . . .

The recital starts. There are two isolated cheers. The singer
looks as she always has looked on record covers and in newspapers; dark-haired, attractive, and unaffected. She has always
sounded pretty much that way, too; and once she begins to
perform, starting her programme with a Scarlatti song, it doesn't
take one long to realize that she still does. Thank God, one tells
oneself as one relaxes: this isn't going to be grotesque. There's
nothing to worry bout. Just sit back, enjoy yourself, and with that
part of yourself that isn't listening to the music, observe the
audience reaction. Are they enthusiastic but critical, like the
Italians? Are they so reserved, so determinedly correct in the
reward they hand out that they sometimes cast a chill on the
performer and thus diminish their own pleasure, as the English
are? Or are they almost too appreciative, cheering practically

everyone and everything, as American audiences tend to be?

To begin with it seems they favour the English approach, though that is perhaps because while the soprano *is* still in excellent condition, there are one or two ragged notes at the bottom, one or two moments when she is clearly having difficulty. But then, as both singer and sung-to get into the spirit of things, and the notes become more secure and the difficulties less obvious, the applause grows warmer and warmer. (Though never reaching, or even approaching, Italian – or American – proportions). Until, after the interval, despite the absence of a bar, and thus of any chance for the audience to drink a bit of enthusiasm into their veins – the atmosphere has become so festive that one song has the whole theatre cheering, and people shouting for more.

Yet it is not Schubert or Brahms that causes this reaction. Nor even Fauré, Richard Strauss, or the fact that the soprano sings it with more intensity than anything else on the programme. No. What has this reserved, homely, Mexican audience applauding so wildly, this white audience that, if it looks back at all, looks back through generations of Mexican born ancestors to Spain, is a Mexican song. And not just any old Mexican song, for there are other pieces by local composers whose performance isn't received with anything like the same degree of excitement. 'To Huey Tlahtzin Cauahtemoc' this one is called, a song whose title, let alone whose words, I suspect not more than five people in the whole theatre understand. If indeed Victoria de los Angeles herself understands it.

Yet somehow it hardly matters. For while those other songs have the names of the poets who wrote the words in brackets after them – Hölty, Claudius, Müller, Rückert, Verlaine, Gautier, Groth, 'To Huey Tlahtzin Cauahtemoc' has something altogether more evocative; something almost guaranteed to make a white middle-class Mexican audience cheer.

Not 'Anonymous'. Not 'Traditional'. Not even, as another does, 'Popular'.

Just two, shortish words.

'Aztec Lament'.

'Brava,' the people shout. 'Brava. Brava. *Brava.*'

For almost a minute.

Tuesday, February 7

From one kind of music to another. Having observed the upper middle-classes in their palace, it is only right – Gerardo tells me – that I see a more popular form of entertainment. He takes me accordingly to Plaza Garibaldi, where the less prosperous and the tourists come, and where the attraction, apart from the many stalls selling fruit, juices, tacos, chickens, and practically every sort of food one could wish for, is the playing of the mariachi bands. These are groups of players from three to fifteen or more, who wear black studded outfits and large hats, who are, far more so than the concert audience, of mixed blood, and who are, for a fee that varies with their number and one's skill at bargaining, for hire. That is, one asks them to play the tune of one's choice; and there, in the middle of the large, crowded square, one listens to it.

But if the audience reaction at the Palacio de Bellas Artes was, on the whole, measured, here it was quite different.

We watched two separate performances. The first was given by a group of five players for a couple of young men; one of whom, as he sat on the edge of a fountain, looked as if he wished the ground would open up and swallow him, while the other, his brother or his friend, appeared quite at ease, and with a slightly idiotic expression simply gazed about him, beaming. And the second, a more elaborate affair, was given by a fifteen man band for a family group consisting of grandparents, parents, children, and assorted unclassifiable adults, all of whom, as they sat on a pair of benches or on the ground beneath, remained still and quiet for as long as the music lasted: frozen, as if they were having their photograph taken with a very slow exposure.

What was remarkable about the reaction of the two young men and the family group – not to mention the many onlookers who assisted at the show – was the fact that when the music finished, and the guitars and trumpets and accordions were lowered, no one, neither those who had paid for the show, nor those who were standing around, gave any sign of appreciation whatsoever. The young men merely got up from their perch on the edge of the fountain and drifted off. And the members of the family merely unfroze and started moving again, talking to each other, sorting out sweaters and children, and tearing with their fingers at great pink sticks of spun sugar; that broke off in soft wispy lumps and stuck to their chins as they tried to cram it into their mouths, or broke into smaller fluffier pieces that floated earthwards to attach themselves to legs, or trousers, or shoes. Not a clap was given, not a word of thanks, not, other than incidentally, a glance of acknowledgement. It was as if the musicians had never existed, or as if someone else had been listening to them. And when a thin tightly curled American woman standing by her large flower-shirted husband expressed her enthusiasm, one felt suddenly embarrassed for her, as for someone who had unwittingly burped in church, or infringed a taboo whose existence she hadn't been aware of.

Tonight, just a single 'Bravo', and one takes a step back.

Tourist, tourist, one mutters, as one dissolves oneself in the crowd . . .

Not that the musicians themselves appeared upset by the lack of response; obviously they were used to it. They just put their instruments down and started talking to each other as if they too had not had any contact with the people who had, until a moment ago, been listening to them. All the same, one couldn't help wishing that the transaction had inspired joy in at least one of the parties to it; as one couldn't, equally, help wondering what life must have been like for these musicians. Playing day after day after day, and never knowing whether any of the people they were playing for liked their music; or, indeed, heard it. Week after week, month after month, year after year, with only the occasional American tourist making a blunder, and calling out a tentative 'Bravo'.

Like a painter painting paintings for the blind, or a singer singing songs for the deaf.

It must have been depressing, it seemed to me, and that was why, when Gerardo asked me if I wanted to eat and have a drink here or somewhere else, I said 'somewhere else'. Still, as I say, they didn't look unduly depressed, those guitarists and accordionists, and even as we left they were still calling out hopefully to me, trying to get me to hire them.

'Oye, güero,' they cried. 'Güero.' Which means: fair-haired man.

But I said no to all of them, or walked on by without replying. As if they didn't exist; or I hadn't, really, heard them.

*

We went to a vast, almost deserted bar to have our beer, and some fish soup, and cheese-filled tortillas. And there, sitting at a table, while the few other clients of the place played dominoes, and the many, elderly waiters stood around in their white jackets, gazing at the emptiness, I told the story of how I had first heard that word 'Güero'; or, more exactly, 'Güerote'. Which means: tall fair man.

I had gone with Enrique to Tula, about fifty miles north of Mexico City, because I wanted to see the Toltec Atlantes – four monumental temple columns in stylized human form that figure on half the postage stamps and posters of Mexico – and because the Toltecs, and Tula, played an important part in the propagation of the myth of Quetzalcoatl; a myth which itself has played an important part in the history of Mexico.

The Toltecs, who were probably a branch of the Chichimec Indians (Chichimec meaning 'sons of bitches', and actually being a generic name for all warlike nomadic Indians from the north), though possibly of Celtic or Irish descent, established themselves from around 700 A.D. as a distinctive cultural force. From 900 to 1300 they were the dominant tribe in Mesoamerica, their influence extending down to the Yucatan Peninsula. They had adopted Quetzalcoatl, the Plumed Serpent and the god of civilization, from the Teotihuacans, whose city of more than two hundred thousand people had been thirty miles to the south and east of Tula. But in the middle of the tenth century, Ce Acatl Topiltzin, the son of the Toltec leader and a priest, not only set up the Toltec capital in Tula, but, as a patron of the arts, and as a pacifist, began to be thought of either as the mouthpiece of Quetzalcoatl, or as the incarnation of Quetzalcoatl; the god made flesh. He was, apparently – hence the legend of his people's Irish or Celtic provenance? – a fair-haired man with a beard, and when, after a power struggle with a more warlike faction at court, he was banished from Tula and moved south first to Cholula and then to Chichen Itza – a small Maya town that he transformed into the grandest ceremonial centre in Mesoamerica – he passed, at the same time, into legend. He died, one story went, by setting himself alight in his feathered cloak, and flying up to heaven to become the morning star. But another more potent story was that he sailed off into the east: from where, it was predicted – in the year 1519 to be precise – he would return.

In 1519 Hernan Cortes landed in the northern tip of Yucatan . . .

It was to this place, then (that had been sacked by other Chichimecas – possibly Mexicas, who would later be called Aztecs – in the twelfth century) that I came one afternoon, having driven up from Mexico City. We parked the car near the dusty central square of the small rather run-down town and asked how to get to 'the ruins'.

Down here, along a bit, across a bridge and you're there.

Fine, we said, thank you, and set off. It was a hot dry day, and as we walked 'down here' – which turned out to be an unpaved street of one-storey buildings with open doors – it was difficult not to wonder whether the story of Topiltzin/Quetzalcoatl's predicted return was a legend that the Spanish had exploited, if not indeed invented, for their own ends – to give their conquest a mythic dimension. It was also hard not to feel, assuming the legend did already exist, that it must have been the primary factor in Moctezuma's defeat; what caused him to prevaricate, and put off attacking and destroying Cortes when he could have, and thus bring about his own death and the destruction of his empire. Of course those historians who maintained that it was the com- bination of Spanish gunpowder, Spanish horses, and other Aztec-hating Indians that brought about Moctezuma's downfall were probably correct in theory. And undoubtedly if Cortes had been destroyed it would only have been a matter of time before some other Spaniards or some other Europeans had invaded and overthrown Moctezuma; for by 1519 the Aztecs were, according to prevailing European standards, a cultural anomaly; which is only one step away from cultural irrelevance, and non- existence.

Yet as I peered nervously into those small open houses and shops, tried to imagine what it must be like to live in a place like this, and felt my wallet to reassure myself that if I wanted to I could be back in Europe in just twelve hours or so, theories did not really satisfy. They didn't have the ring of truth. They lacked poetry. Whereas the myth of a returning pale god who brings – albeit with the sword – civilization; that was more satis- factory. Yes, I told myself: *that's* it. For isn't poetry, ultimately, always more truthful than mere 'fact?' And if it hadn't been for Moctezuma's failure of will maybe the Spanish *wouldn't* have won. After all – the Japanese didn't have gunpowder until the beginning of this century, and *they* were never defeated.

That the civilization the returning god brought was of doubtful benefit to Moctezuma and his countrymen was, as far as this argument was concerned, neither here nor there. The king couldn't have foreseen that he would be killed, that his city would be torn down, and that his people would be virtually enslaved for the next three hundred years . . .

'Oye,' a small boy shouted at me as I walked along, day-dreaming in this fashion, and added something else. Something I thought had probably been 'Gringo', and something which, as a result, instantly pulled me up and reminded me I was living in the threatening present; a foreigner in a distant land.

You are a representative of the hated invader, the crumbling walls muttered. Of the burner of temples and the razer of cities. Of the enslaver.

I expected a stone to hit my head. Or a dollop of spit . . .

But when I looked at the small dark boy – some ten yards back now, and sitting on the sidewalk, I saw he was smiling and waving at me. So I smiled and waved back, and relaxed.

'What,' I said to Enrique 'did he say?'

'Güerote,' Enrique said. 'Oye, güerote.'

'Which means?'

'Tall fair man.'

'And it isn't an insult?'

'No,' Enrique shook his head. 'Not at all.'

I laughed. 'I thought I was about to be attacked.'

'Don't be stupid. Did he look like the sort of person who would attack you? He's only eight years old.'

'Yes, I know, but –'

You can never tell in a distant land, I thought, as we rounded the corner; and, looking back one final time, the child gave another wave.

And though I wouldn't have liked it if it had been an insult, if the boy had seen me as a representative of the hated invader – well, I assured myself, I suppose I would have understood.

As it was I walked on towards the hill where the temple had once stood, muttering 'Güerote, Güerote,' under my breath, and feeling, suddenly – and absurdly – pleased with myself.

As if I had been turned, for a moment, into a god.

Wednesday, February 8

An afternoon spent with Mr F; and an evening spent with both Mr and Mrs F.

In the afternoon Mr F took me round the university where he teaches, showing me the faculty buildings of Architecture and Biology, Chemistry and Dentistry, and so on through E F G and H to the Z of Zoology ('Er – mmm – Yes,' I murmured, appreciative of the tour but not certain what to say other than that the campus was vast and well-kept and pretty much like every other campus I had ever seen). And from there we went on to some new shopping complex, where we wandered round in a semi-daze from store to store, department to department ('Er – mmm – Yes,' I murmured, in front of the bed-linen, silver-ware, children's toys, costume jewellery, china, and ladies underwear, 'It's all very well displayed, isn't it?') before ending up in a branch of Sanborns – a chain of restaurants, coffee-shops and department stores – having tea and waffles in an oppressive carpeted tea-room that made me feel slightly hysterical. (The waitresses, in ersatz Indian costumes with long skirts and yellow wings, wouldn't come to take our order; while the other clients exuded an air of over-dressed over-coiffed smugness. And as I tried not to yawn, and tried to distinguish his voice from all the others, Mr F explained to me, at great length and in great detail, why and to what extent, Einstein's theory of relativity was wrong. 'Er – mmm – Yes,' I said, and thought, I've got to get out of here.)

The evening, however, was even more of a strain.

Luckily I had put on a suit and tie before coming out, instead of my usual old sweater and jeans, because the restaurant that Mr and Mrs F took me to was of a sort that didn't allow one in unless one was wearing a suit and tie. But once we were past the various doormen and hat-check girls and receptionists at the entrance, in fact what one was wearing became almost immaterial, since the restaurant, built on the edge of a lake in the middle of Chapultepec Park, and one of the most expensive in the city, was so dark that one would have had difficulty in making out even the shabbiest pair of jeans, even the dirtiest of sweaters.

We were shown to a table by a waiter who spoke English to Mr F.

The place was full. Ninety to ninety-five per cent of those

present were Americans. And though the view of the lake – and of the fountains in the lake – was grand, conversation or even communication was practically impossible. Still more than in Sanborns tea-room, all the sound congealed into a sort of bruise of noise, in which it was difficult to distinguish any individual voice.

Why do people come here, one wonders in such places. What makes this restaurant so crowded? It can't just be the view. And it certainly isn't the food. So why . . . ?

The answer, I concluded, as I leaned forward and put my ear to Mr F's mouth – to hear him tell me that Chapultepec Park had once been an Aztec game reserve, and that the castle that dominated it had been Maximilian's royal residence – is that although all these people, so prosperous, so apparently cheerful, so solid and well-dressed and confident, look as if they wouldn't flinch before a lion, they are all, to differing degrees, in one respect at least, like me. That is – despite their appearance, and though most would deny it – they are fearful. And they come here because, irrespective of the quality of the food, and irrespective of the fact that they can't hear their companions – and that the seats aren't terribly comfortable, and the whole atmosphere is about as conducive to relaxation as an airport waiting-room – they feel safe. Here, in the gloom, surrounded by waiters, with the palm-trees growing to the ceiling, and the knowledge that they are not going to be disturbed by any sight of the poor, the hungry, or the rebellious – indeed, by the sight of anything except the glint of gold in the darkness, and the flickering of the occasional candle, and the illuminated fountain in the lake – they can be at ease.

And that, I told myself, as I ate my cold avocado soup, my unknown fish cooked in an unknown sauce, my not quite fresh fruit salad, is what civilization is all about. That is why we fight and play music. That is why we kill and write books. That is why we try to convince others that our way is a better way, and used to attempt to convert the heathen.

To keep ourselves safe.

Safe from disorder. Safe from hunger, death and disease. Safe – from the Indians . . .

One has no alternative but to hold conversations with oneself, when it is so hard to hold them with others.

'Thank you,' I told the F's when they finally dropped me off

outside my house. 'Thank you so much.' And despite everything, I was not being insincere; since I was, as usual, grateful to
them for their generosity and kindness. All the more grateful
because I had a sense – also, it seemed, as usual with them – of
guilt; for having spent my whole evening – not to mention most of
my afternoon – feeling so uncomfortable.

But I was, as I got out of the car, turned, and waved to them,
very relieved that the day was over; and began to wonder
whether I was so keen on safety as I thought. I mean it's all very
well, I told myself, putting the key in the lock, but perhaps one
can take it too far . . .

'Oh, Hugh,' Mrs F called from the car. 'By the way – Patty's
coming on Saturday. 'Phone us.'

And that, I reflected as I waved again and pushed the door
open, was something else to think about.

Thursday, February 9

Just now, when I went to buy the newspaper in my local branch of
Sanborns, I passed a shoe-shine stand. There was a pasty-faced,
overweight young executive-type in a not very well-fitting brown
suit sitting in the raised chair, having his ankle boots cleaned. The
shoe-shine boy was an old white-haired man. Nevertheless,
despite his shape and his suit, and his pock-marked skin, moth-
eaten moustache, plump damp hands and pale shifty eyes, there
was something rather appealing about the young man; something that made me feel warmly towards him. Perhaps it was
because his weak stray-dog eyes looked helpless, and innocent,
and vulnerable. Or perhaps it was because as he sat there on
Avenida Insurgentes, with the traffic fumes making the morning
misty, he seemed quite unembarrassed; to be clutching a single,
long-stemmed, perfect pink rose.

Thursday afternoon

A question.

If I didn't like Georgina last time I was here, and she didn't like
me, why did I go to see her this afternoon? My having told myself
in London that I might look her up had been before I had heard
from Gerardo, and before I had thought I would land on my feet.

And I certainly wasn't expecting to see a helpless, innocent or vulnerable expression in her eye.

Well, there were two reasons. One was that Enrique had assured me that we had both changed in the years since we had met, and that he thought we might get on well together now. And the other more cynical reason was that though I had landed on my feet for the moment, I knew that Georgina had a car and a certain amount of free time. If we did get on better together this time, I thought, I might be able to persuade her to take a trip with me when I set off again on my travels, once Gerardo had started back at the University. Obviously if she can't, or doesn't want to, take any time off work, or if we still don't like each other, I will have to go by myself, taking trains, or buses, or planes. But if she would like to come with me it will make life much easier and pleasanter. I can go exactly where I want to go, see exactly what I want to see, and above all do both without having to haul bags around, sweating through strange cities looking for hotels or sitting in the main square of small towns wondering if there is a hotel at all.

I thought around four-thirty might be a good time to find her in. Enrique had told me that she worked at the television – as a script-writer – in the mornings, and I assumed that she would have lunch at home. (Lunchtime in Mexico being between two-thirty and five). But since she had no telephone I had to go round and ring her doorbell. (In fact she had no doorbell.)

She lives just south of the Paseo de la Reforma – a wide tree-lined avenue of hotels and airline offices built in imitation of the Champs-Elysees in Paris – in an area that is, though only two blocks away from the bright lights, slightly seedy and crumbling and sad. And her building, too – five storeys high, green, and with broken glass in some of the windows – has seen better days.

As I approached the green iron street door, a woman, leaning out of a window directly above, shouted who did I want.

Apartment eight, I told her.

'Momentito,' she called down, 'I'll come down and open for you.'

Actually it was her small and pale-faced daughter who opened the door, and who informed me, with a nod of the head, that I wanted the second floor.

'Gracias,' I told her, and glanced apprehensively around the shabby, broken-tiled hallway, which looked more dirty than in reality it was. I headed towards the stairs, as the noise of children playing in the covered court round which the apartments were built echoed up the stairwell, and made the place even sound harsh and dismal and mean. It was cold there I noted, and shivered.

But when, having knocked three times on the bell-less door, it was opened by a small, dark-haired, and rather intense looking young woman whom I no more recognized than she did me, and who said, tentatively, 'Hugh?' just as I said, tentatively, 'Georgina?', I started to feel better. For not only was it obvious, with the first words we exchanged, that we were going to get on well together, but the very fact that neither of us remembered the other seemed to augur well. We must indeed have changed, I told myself, as I went in, Georgina closed the door behind me, and she offered me a beer. Changed beyond all recognition . . .

We spent almost three hours together, testing the water as it were. At the end of three hours Georgina asked me if I would like to go with her to have drinks with two Americans she had to meet, and I asked her if by any chance she could or would take some time off, and wanted, by any further chance, to drive round the Bajio with me – an area north of Mexico City that included the cities of San Miguel de Allende, Guanajuato, and Querétaro.

'I will pay all the expenses,' I said, 'but if you'd like to come . . .'

Georgina smiled. 'Oh yes,' she said; she'd love to come. You see – just yesterday she'd quit her job.

There was, it seemed to me, a pattern in things. First Gerardo's Christmas card. Now Georgina's convenient freedom.

What was she going to do, I asked her as we drove, not very far, into the Zona Rosa; the principal tourist part of town.

Well, she said, she wasn't too sure, but what she'd like to do was return to Italy, where she had spent some time the year before learning Italian, and where she had been very happy.

Oh, Italy, Italy, Italy, she said.

And Mexico?

There was no future for her in the cinema in Mexico, she told me. As a matter of fact, there was no Mexican cinema. And as all her life she had wanted to work in movies, and had only worked with television to get experience for working in movies . . . That was why she had quit yesterday. To force herself to make a move.

'Have you ever *seen* a Mexican movie?' she asked me.

'Well only the ones Bunuel made here, but . . .'

'They're not Mexican. They're Bunuel. Mexican movies – without exception, are the worst movies in the whole world. They're incredible. And they're not getting any better. You know the last President, Lopez Portillo? He appointed his sister – his *sister* – as head of the National Film Board. A woman who knew no more about making films than – than her brother did about honesty. And that's the way things are here. Either the films are American – or they're unwatchable. So the only thing to do *is* leave. Go to Italy. Go to France. Go to England. Go anywhere I can work. Just to get away from here.'

'And the States?'

'I don't like America,' Georgina said.

'Why not?'

'I don't know. Well I mean I do, but – oh, you know.'

Do I?

I suspect that in the States, Georgina is afraid of being made to feel like – or simply of feeling like – a Third World person, and a second class citizen. Whereas here, from the very way she holds herself, from the very way she talks, and from the very look of her face, that is both pale and Mediterranean, one can tell, immediately, that she is a first class citizen. And likes it.

'The Indians? They are nothing to do with me. *Nothing*.'

'And if,' I ask her, 'you can't work in Europe?'

'I don't know. But . . . I've got to. I will. I've just got to get away. I mean I love Mexico. I love the climate, the food, my friends, the flowers – but you can't live on flowers, can you? Perhaps it's because I'm from the north of Mexico. We're different up there. But oh, who knows. But I would like to go back to Italy. They've got it both there.'

'Both what?'

'Well – both the climate *and* something to do. Both . . . both . . .'

Both flowers and dreams?

'You know.'

'Yes,' I said, 'I do.' And this time I was sure I did. I had lived in Italy myself for thirteen years . . .

'Though I'm not sure if it's true any more. I'm not sure if it's true anywhere in Europe any more. I mean it's probably still truer in the north of Europe than in the South. But even there – you really should go to the States,' I said, 'if you want to work.'

'Yes, I know. But if I really don't like it – oh well, something'll turn up, and at least I've done the important thing, which is given up my job here.'

'Important for me, if you're going to drive me round!'

'And even if I don't get to Italy – oh well,' she repeated, 'I'm sorry. I don't want to bore you with my problems.'

'That's all right,' I said. 'I'm always having the same discussion with myself. Whether to stay in England. Whether to go back to Italy. Or whether to try to go to the States. But what I don't understand is – if you've just quit your job, and you don't like Americans – what are we going to see some Americans for?'

'Oh,' Georgina said, 'because I translated something one of them wrote and is trying to sell to the television here. And I want to get paid. And, because there's the possibility that there might be some more work. Which I'm going to need.'

'By the way,' she added as she parked the car, 'they're homosexuals.'

*

Indeed they were; and – which was perhaps what Georgina had meant – they were very little else. They were hardly Americans; they were hardly a television script-writer and a doctor; they were hardly, really, anything. Simply – homosexuals. To break the ice, so to speak, as we sat in the large, damp, underfurnished and over-priced apartment they had rented for a month, they complained – directing their remarks with almost personal animosity towards Georgina – about how they had been gypped by their landlady. 'She counted every knife and fork in the place when we took it,' muttered the writer, a tall man of around forty with greying hair and a grey face, whose voice was slightly slurred as if he had had a stroke or were on drugs. 'And when we pointed out that one of the lavatories didn't work she turned right round and said that maybe we could fix it. "Perhaps you know how these things work." *Bitch.*' They also complained, a little later, about how they had been gypped by the telephone repair man. 'When we moved in the telephone wasn't working as it was meant to be. So we called and some guy came round and sold us a new one. Only when *that* didn't work either, and we called again, the second guy said that the new 'phone wasn't new at all, and that anyway we shouldn't have paid for it.' And throughout our visit, in little asides here and there, they complained how everything in this country was dirty, slovenly, bureaucratic, stupid and inefficient. 'Back home we're used to things *working*.' But these complaints were simply ice-breakers, asides. For they spent most of their time – still directing nearly all their remarks at Georgina, though with even greater animosity now – talking about just one thing. Their sex lives. About how they picked up boys here. About how much – or how little – they paid their boys here. About how they treated their boys here. ('You've got to tell them what to do all the time,' said the doctor, who was as short and plump and dark – and, in a cold way, bright – as his companion was tall and grey and dull. 'Never let them doubt that you're in charge.') And – and here sex and complaining merged – again and again, about how stupid their boys were here. 'They're so *ignorant*,' slurred Tall, shaking his head at the thought. 'It's as if – they've got no inner life.'

'They *have* got no inner life.'

'They're so spiritless. So empty. So . . . dumb. I mean they're sweet. Very sweet. But . . .'

'You know what the real trouble is, don't you?' laughed the doctor – looking at Tall but giving a glance at Georgina – 'they're Mexican. That's all it is. They were born here. They grew up here. They're *Mexican*.'

For half an hour it went on, for an hour, as Georgina sat there nodding and refusing to be either shocked or antagonized, and as I got so bored and cold and depressed that I started to fall asleep. Why do you come here, I wanted to ask them, if you despise the place and its people so much? (And they did come often, apparently. Two or three times a year.) Why does Tall want to have his work put on television here? And why why why, when you could presumably be happy, are you so hostile, so mean-spirited, and so contemptuous? But I didn't ask, of course. I simply concentrated on trying not to look too hostile – towards them – myself – after all, Georgina really might need some more work from them – and trying not to fall asleep entirely.

'What you need,' muttered Tall, 'is another drink.'

'Oh no I don't,' I said just managing to smile. 'I'll pass out here if I do. In fact,' I went on, trying to catch Georgina's eye, 'I think I must be going.'

'Oh stay for a little bit longer,' said Tall. 'It's early yet. It's only just past eleven.'

'I know, but I have to get up early in the morning, and –'

'I guess we must like it here really,' Short suddenly said to Georgina, as if he hadn't heard my preparations for departure. Or as if, having heard them, he felt that maybe he had gone too far, and should in some way apologize to the only Mexican present. 'Otherwise we wouldn't keep on coming. Perhaps if we saw more of the country . . .'

'Why haven't you?' said Georgina, getting up herself. 'Why've you never driven here?'

'We've thought about it,' sighed Tall, as he realized we really were going, and slowly lifted himself from his chair, 'but it's such a long way. And besides, we've heard the highways are dangerous.'

'Dangerous? You only have to drive slowly when you're going through villages. And be careful of dogs and donkeys.'

'Oh it isn't donkeys we're scared of,' laughed Short, as he, defiantly, stayed seated. 'It's bandits.'

'*Bandits?*'

'Yeah. We've heard there are bandits on the roads. That's why we've never come down by car. But maybe, one day – if we bring the dogs . . .'

'Goodbye,' I said, 'and thank you.'

Short nodded from his chair, and still didn't move as his friend accompanied us to the door.

'You're the first Englishman I've ever met who didn't drink like a fish,' Tall said, shaking my hand.

'Yes?' I told him, and then, as I couldn't think what else to say, 'Oh.'

'Do come and see us again when you have time. We do like to speak English you know. And as we're here for another month . . .'

It was cold on the balcony outside the apartment, and Georgina and I shivered and started to walk away even while Tall was still speaking.

'Any time. We're always at home. Just ring on the door. Any time.'

'Goodnight,' we said, as we looked around, to see Tall framed against the light in his doorway, looking tired, and thin, and old. 'And thanks again for the drink.'

'Sure,' he said. 'Thanks for coming. And thank you Georgina for the translation.'

'That's okay. We'll be in touch.'

'Sure.'

'Goodnight.'

'Goodnight.'

Goodnight . . .

'Bandits,' Georgina laughed, when we got down the stairs, and let ourselves out into the crowded, brightly-lit street. 'Bandits! I mean – really.' She shook her head. 'They're mad.'

'They certainly are. But didn't you get offended when they were going on like that about Mexico?'

'No. What's the point? Anyway, at least he paid.' She laughed again. 'If he'd been Mexican he probably wouldn't even have paid. So – do you want a lift home?'

'No,' I said, 'I don't think so thanks. They depressed me. I think I'm going to walk. I need some air.'

'You know the way?'

'I think so. Straight down Insurgentes, no?'

'Yes.'

'Good. Well – I'll be round some time in the next day or two. And Monday – off to San Miguel.'

'Monday or Tuesday.'

'Whenever.'

'I'm sorry about tonight.'

'Oh that's all right. Just one of those things. And at least it didn't go on for too long.'

'Long enough!'

'That's true. Anyway – look after yourself, sleep well, and – it's good to see you again.'

Georgina knew what I meant, and smiled. 'Yes, and it's good to see you again, too. But go straight home now, and be careful of the bandits.'

'I will. Don't worry. I'm always careful of bandits.'

'Talk to you tomorrow.'

'Or Saturday.'
'Or Sunday.'
'Goodnight.'
'Goodnight.'
Goodnight . . .

*

Though the Zona Rosa was still crowded, by the time I got onto Insurgentes, the avenue that crosses Reforma, and runs from north to south of the city, there was no one about. And either because I was still tired and depressed, or, more probably, because I was just my normally apprehensive self, that word 'bandits' came back to me as I hurried along, and I wasn't able to smile at it quite so readily. Obviously I don't mean bandits as such, I told myself, putting my hands in my jacket pocket to keep them warmer. I mean – that's an absurd notion. But you are in a city of seventeen million people an unknown number of whom don't really have enough to eat. And you have heard stories of muggings, and kidnappings. So maybe you should have accepted Georgina's offer of a ride home, and maybe you shouldn't now be out on this wide empty street where there's not another pedestrian to be seen. Because you are clearly a foreigner, and you are, therefore, presumed not to be poor – however much you may aspire to invisibility by wearing old blue jeans, an old blue sweater, and an old blue jacket.

Resisting the temptation to take a taxi, I continued on past the shoe shops, the wedding dress shops, and the closed and shuttered taco stands.

Cars sped by.

It was cold.

I walked faster.

Bandits . . .

Friday, February 10

If you take Reforma going west, passing the Maria-Isabel Sheraton and various other shining glass high-rises, and crossing Chapultepec Park, you start climbing; and come, fairly soon, to Las Lomas, where behind high white walls and fancy wrought iron fencing, the rich live in their large white villas, or their ornate turn-of-the-century mansions. The grass verges are carefully tended here, the bougainvillaea is particularly bright and abundant, and the air is cleaner than in the city below.

Gerardo lives in Las Lomas, in what is virtually a one room apartment attached to the side of one of these villas. He rents it from an old Dutch woman, Mrs B – she who loaned us the car. The room is rather cheap, since Mrs B, who occupies the main house, is otherwise alone, and likes to have someone near; and the disadvantages of the zone – the near absence of public transport (it being assumed that if you live here you will have your own transport) and the scarcity of shops (it being assumed your maid will have her own transport too) are outweighed both by the – comparative – cleanliness of the air, and by the fact that Mrs B, her generosity with the car apart, is, as Gerardo puts it, 'entertaining.' By which he means she has a good fund of stories.

It was to meet Mrs B – and to see the neighbourhood – that Gerardo invited me up to Las Lomas yesterday afternoon. 'Come and have tea,' he said. 'And some cakes.'

In fact we ended up drinking rum with the landlady.

Mrs B is in her eighties; a handsome, erect, white-haired old woman, who is clearly nobody's fool. She was born in Mexico, near Oaxaca, where her father had a coffee plantation.

('It was the best run coffee plantation in the whole of Oaxaca. Maybe in the whole of Mexico. Which is why it was the first place that was taken over in the revolution in 1910. We lost *everything*.'

Well, not quite everything, since aside from this – in comparison with its neighbours – merely fair-sized house, Mrs B owns two other larger houses just down the road. Also the floors, in the living room, study, dining room bedroom and hallway, are covered with very beautiful Persian and Indian carpets, the furniture – 'We bought some of it from Europe, the rest is colonial' – is, whatever its origin, magnificent, and there are cabinets filled with what looks like, and almost certainly is, Chinese porcelain of great value and, again, very great beauty.)

Yet though she was born here, only spending a few years in Holland as a girl, and though she is fiercely patriotic ('You are writing a book about Mexico? You must only say good things, you understand that. This is a wonderful country. This is the only country on earth. We do not like people speaking badly about Mexico, do we Gerardo? *We will not hear a word against it.*') she has always retained her Dutch passport. And despite her admonitions and her love of Mexico, one suspects that in the final analysis her true allegiances lie elsewhere. Or at best her feelings are mixed.

She tells us, as we sit sipping our rum, and I make a tentative effort at friendship with a suspicious and, in his mistress's words, funny-tempered dachshund, a tale . . .

'I love America,' she says. 'That is the United States. My son lives there, and my grandchildren, and – I have always loved it. And the Americans, too. So last year, before the elections – I thought I would move there. Because I thought – here is going to be a revolution, and they will take everything away. And – I packed up everything. All the silver. All the porcelain. All the furniture. Everything I had accumulated in my life. It took weeks. Weeks. And when everything was ready – off I went to Texas. I stayed with my son for a few months. And then I bought a place of my own. In Dallas. It was beautiful. A penthouse. I unpacked everything and the shippers had done a wonderful job. Not a thing was missing. Not a thing was broken. But it was very tiring. The move. The change, after all this time. And then one afternoon when everything was finally done I thought – Thank God. And now I'm going to have a rest. So I went to bed and fell asleep.

'When I woke up I heard something moving in my living room.

'I got up and went to the door. I didn't have any shoes on, so I didn't make any noise.

'The janitor of the building, who had my keys of course, and had been helping me with the move, was going through my handbag, which was lying on the piano. I suppose I should have just gone back to bed – there wasn't much money in it. But I didn't think, and anyway, it was, how do you say? instinctive. I said "What are you doing?" The poor man, he was so shocked – he didn't realize I was in the house – panicked. He came over to me – he hit me in the face – and then he tried to strangle me. I mean – he did strangle me. I thought Oh dear – to have left Mexico to end up being strangled by the janitor. Then I lost consciousness. He thought I was dead. Luckily. When I came to I called the police and they came round and arrested him. Poor man,' she repeated, 'it was so stupid. For twenty, thirty dollars. The police wanted me to press charges of course. But it would have meant I had to stay there. And after that – all I wanted to do was get back to my beloved Mexico.' (The elections were over by now, Gerardo told me afterwards. And no revolution had broken out.) 'And so I hired a firm of shippers – and flew back. And now – here I am again. Still unpacking. Still trying to find things. Because I tell you, the American shippers are not so efficient as the Mexicans. The Americans haven't just lost one of my vases. They have lost a sofa, too. I mean to say – how do you lose a *sofa*? But I tell you – I am so happy to be back. And now, I am not moving again. Whatever happens. War. Revolution. They can take everything away. But at least I am here in my own home. In Mexico. And no one is going to strangle me. And even if they do – I prefer a Mexican strangler. You know what I mean? I do not want to be strangled in a strange land. Don't misunderstand me. As I say, I love America. And I know not all Americans are stranglers. But . . .'

She got up and straightened a silver framed photograph of one of her children, and then led us back into the dining-room where the rest of her silver was spread out on the table.

'But I am so tired, you know that. Packing. Unpacking. Moving. Moving back. I said to Gerardo the other day – I'm going to unpack all these things and then, when everything's ready – I'm going to die. I've had enough. I mean – what is the point? I am old, I am tired – I told you that, didn't I Gerardo?'

'Yes,' Gerardo agreed, 'you did.'

'And I mean it. I am sick of the whole business. It is no *fun* being old and – you want another rum?'

'No thank you,' said Gerardo, and 'I think we must be going,' said Fleetwood.

'All my friends are dead, my husband's dead – what are you doing tonight?'

'Going to the opera. To see *Tosca*.'

'With Domingo?'

'No. Domingo's singing next week.'

'Oh, he has a great voice. A great voice. And he was brought up here too, you know. Oh well – it was nice to meet you, and I hope we will meet again.'

'I hope so.'

'And remember, write nice things about Mexico.'

'I'll try to.'

'You mustn't try. You must do it. Mustn't he Gerardo?'

'Yes,' said Gerardo, 'Of course.'

'Because there are lots of things wrong with this country. But only we're allowed to say so. If anyone else does – we get very angry.'

'I'll remember,' I smile.

'Please do,' Mrs B said waving a finger at me, and also semi-smiling. 'Otherwise we'll start saying bad things about England, and then you'll get offended. So –'

We left her standing amidst her silver, shaking her head and wondering what to do next.

But though she was old and her unpacking, it seemed, was almost done, she didn't, despite her sighs, look at all tired or in the least bit ready to go.

Indeed, bright-eyed and firm-handed, she looked good certainly for another ten years, and probably for several more. And having survived revolution in her early life, and strangulation in her late, one suspected that it would take more than an attack of 'oh-what's-the-point?'s to carry her off. After all, even when the silver was sorted out there was still a sofa to be traced. And when the sofa turned up – or the insurance money came through – there'd still be this thought to keep an old woman going. That – interest in children and grandchildren apart – weariness of the soul had never been one of the characteristics of the Dutch interior.

*

Going back into town on one of the infrequent buses, and peering from our vantage point over the high bougainvillaea covered walls:

'Have you noticed,' Gerardo said, 'how most of the people up here are fair?'

*

And so, as I sat through a performance of *Tosca*, listening to a tired strained tenor and a fat little butter ball of a soprano who was, despite her shape, her tendency to overact, and her inability to move without getting her six-inch platform heels caught in the hem of her red velvet dress, actually rather good, I perceived through the loud and gutsily played music that a theme was starting to emerge from my experiences of the past few days. And that a figure was moving into the foreground of my picture, demanding to be painted.

It was undeniable, I told myself, that social and economic distinctions in this country split, by and large, along racial lines. By no means exclusively, and less and less so; indeed in another hundred years it might not be true at all. Nevertheless, for the moment, the general rule was that the whiter you were, the more of Spanish or other European descent you were, the higher you were likely to be in the social and economic scale. And the more Indian you were, the more your face and language proclaimed your descent from Olmec, Maya, Zapotec or Aztec forebears, the lower you were likely to be on the scale. Until, in those villages in the south where Spanish wasn't spoken at all, and in those canyons in the north where the inhabitants still lived by hunting – as if ten thousand years of history had never taken place – you were almost not on the scale at all. (Like those who were most discriminated against in any country. The difference here being that in Mexico, however much one might be at the bottom of the heap, and however much one might not wish to be in the heap at all, there were others not only determined to see one as part of the social structure, but determined to see the whole social structure as resting on one. Determined in fact to see one as the foundation of the structure. As, in a sense, one was. Though it was ironic that those who did wish to consider the Indians in such a light were generally those with the highest perch, those who could peer down from some intellectual pent-house into the mud huts and canyon floors, and say with pink lips – as they pointed with white hands – 'Those are the real Mexicans.')

But if this were the case, I went on, as Tosca sang that she had lived for art and love, then wasn't it risky for someone of European descent to come here? Risky primarily for 'the soul', but risky also, ultimately, for the body?

Yes, I told myself, it was. For the temptation was obvious. Either to make the equation 'European equals civilized', and to forget how that civilization was imposed, and how it was maintained. Or to reduce the matter to one of mere aesthetics, and make the equation 'white equals civilized'; thus crossing the border into the territory of crude racial prejudice.

Though generally when people say the former, they mean the latter.

The emergence of this theme – or rather the reminder that such a theme can constantly be heard in the background in Mexico – because I had been aware of it before, as much as I had been of the landscape – and the stepping into the light of a pale figure muttering 'My way is *the* way,' was what made me start to think that my agent had been right to warn me of the dangers of Mexico; even if he hadn't meant quite a danger of this sort. But as the opera proceeded, it occurred to me that the temptation to make the European, or 'white equals civilized' equation was not the only danger inherent in the 'Indian problem' that existed here. There was another that was, perhaps, still greater; though I hesitated for a while before naming it.

This second temptation, and this greater danger, was, it seemed to me, the way that Mexico encourages the visitor or the Mexican of European descent to be dishonest, to pretend that he or she *doesn't* make at least the first of those equations in his or her head, and pretend that he or she *doesn't* believe that 'European equals civilized'.

At least, I told myself, if one recognizes the nature of the god one worships one can hang back a little – hang back as much as one dares – and whisper and make jokes, if not plot against, the wickedness of gods. One can do as much as one can to limit the power of the ruler in whose country one dwells. But if one denies that one dwells in that country at all – as it is so easy to do in Mexico, where guilt for what has been done to the 'real Mexicans', nostalgia for the apparently splendid past of those real Mexicans, and contempt for the present day rulers (and for practically every ruler since the conquest) all conspire to make one come to such a conclusion – one runs two risks. Either one gives those rulers for whom one has such contempt a free hand – and therefore allows them, and incites them, to become more corrupt, more arrogant, and more contemptible yet. Or one imagines that other rulers, other gods, are not wicked; and gives, unconditionally, all one's allegiance to them.

And thus corrupts them . . .

The opera ended to polite applause, despite the soprano's holding up her arms like a prize-fighter, and acting as if she were being cheered. And as Gerardo and I walked back across the Alameda Park we talked – once again – about 'the Indian problem', and how I felt that it was still the central fact of life here.

The great theme that ran through all of Mexican life, and the figure that had to be placed in the foreground of any portrait of Mexico.

'In other words,' Gerardo said, 'That's what your book is going to be about.'

'Well yes,' I told him. 'Of course. I mean obviously not only. But principally – I suppose it will be. It has to be, it seems to me. If you're going to say anything true about Mexico – you can't avoid it. Or even if you're just going to try to say something true.'

Gerardo nodded. 'I suppose so,' he murmured. Then he smiled and turned to me. 'But have you ever met any Indians?'

I thought. 'No,' I said. 'Not knowingly. Oh sure, in the south – waiters – people in shops – and once – but not really. Not actually known them. No.'

Gerardo nodded again, as if to say 'I thought so.'

'When are you going away with Georgina?'

'Monday or Tuesday.'

'Well if you like – when you come back – I'll take you to meet a family. They don't live in mud huts or anything, but – one of my students is an Indian boy. He's always inviting me up to his village. And I'm sure if I asked him if you could come . . .'

For a moment I had a vision of myself swooping down, as if from a pent-house . . .

'Yes,' I said, 'I'd love to.'

'Good. And that way you'll be able to see – I mean it's not so extraordinary, but there are some Indian style baths there, and – well anyway, call me when you get back, and I'll arrange it all.'

'Thank you,' I said. 'I will.'

'And in the meantime – have a good time, get on well with Georgina, and – by the way, what are you doing tomorrow?'

'Tomorrow?' For a second, so full had my head been of other matters, I couldn't think. Then it came to me. 'Tomorrow,' I told him, 'I'm having lunch with Enrique's cousin.'

'And who,' Gerardo asked, 'is Enrique's cousin?'

'Enrique's cousin,' I said – and the name revived all sorts of memories, as if I had just turned the page of an atlas, and come across a whole part of Mexico that I thought I had forgotten – 'is Patty.'

'Ah,' Gerardo murmured, though the name couldn't have meant anything to him. 'Ah well. Enjoy yourself, see you next week, and say hello to Patty –' this as he turned down the steps of the Metro, and waved over his shoulder in farewell, 'from me.'

'I will,' I told him as I waved back, and prepared, once again, to walk home. 'And – goodnight.'

Bandits, I heard a voice whisper. *Bandits* . . .

But this evening, as I walked, I didn't feel as nervous as I had the night before. Partly, perhaps, because having done it once and survived, I felt confident that I could do it a second time. But more, I suspect, because tonight not only was I not depressed, but I had something other than bandits to think about. I had my other, greater Mexican dangers, for example. And, so to speak, that atlas.

SIX

A Journey In The Past: January 1980

The train to Oaxaca was meant to take twelve hours. But, said the sleeping-car attendant, last week it had taken thirty-six. There had been a landslide on the track, and before they'd been able to clear it –

'Dios mio,' said Patty, and then, looking at the man, who was tall, grey-skinned, and Buster Keaton faced, 'Really?'

'Si senorita,' the attendant nodded mournfully. Didn't we know, the hunch of his shoulders and his whole manner implied, that all Mexican trains ran late? But after a moment he looked up and smiled. 'Si,' he repeated.

'No,' said Patty.

'Si,' he repeated again, more mournfully than ever.

Really?

A slight pause: and then a final 'Si.'

Patty laughed, the man gave another smile, and that was how we left it; the possibility that a train last week had been delayed for twenty-four hours (and the inference that it might happen again) hanging over us, and the probability that it hadn't. But hearing this exchange, and being thus made to feel pleasantly nervous, I suddenly became sure that I was going to enjoy this journey I had embarked on. Until that moment I had been doubtful about setting off for five or six weeks with someone I didn't know very well, and, for the first two or three of those weeks, with someone who, until two days ago, I hadn't met at all. But now, I thought, this may be fun, and became particularly glad that Patty had joined Enrique and me on our journey. Because if I tended to be fearful, Enrique tended to be almost too conscientious and serious as a guide and traveller. With the result that if it had just been the two of us, the trip might have turned into a lecture tour with an apprehensive student and an over intense teacher. As it was, the presence of a third person – particularly of an apparently endlessly cheerful and good-natured third person

– was likely to leaven the dough somewhat, and transform a worthy chore into a pleasure.

Patty hadn't meant to join us. She had come down to Mexico City for a week, from her home town of Hermosillo in the north, where she taught science at the university. But having come, and having heard our plans, she had decided to take two extra weeks off work, and tag along – 'if you don't mind.'

'Mind? Of course not!'

'I've never been to the south,' Patty said. 'And if I don't go now . . .'

We had fixed on Oaxaca as our first stop because Enrique had told me it was one of the most attractive cities in Mexico; and we had decided to go by train both so I could experience a Mexican train ride, and because the journey by road was long, and tiring. But having set off, and having heard what the sleeping-car attendant had to say, we began to wonder if it wouldn't have been better to hire a car, or travel by bus after all – if not to fly – and to wonder further if it might not have been more sensible to go first to the real south – to Yucatan, to Quintana Roo – and then make our way slowly back up north.

'At least that way,' Enrique said, as the train rattled and creaked its way at walking pace through the suburbs of Mexico City – every five minutes or so coming to a halt that one felt might last forever – 'even if we did get held up we'd be heading in the right direction. Whereas this way . . .'

But now was too late for such considerations. And after we had decided that Enrique and Patty would share the one private room we had managed to book, while I would try to get some rest in the communal sleeping car, we ate the dinner we had prepared and packed before leaving, we killed the cockroach that Patty found under her seat, and I went, quite glad I was in the communal car, to read something about my destination. So that I wouldn't arrive entirely unprepared in a city whose name I hadn't even heard of until a week ago, and certainly hadn't known how to pronounce.

'Oaxaca,' I read, stretched out on my bunk behind a rusty brown curtain, and wondering whether to keep my wallet in my pocket or hide it under the mattress, 'is the capital of the state of Oaxaca. It is the birthplace of two of Mexico's most famous presidents, Benito Juárez and Porfirio Díaz, though Oaxaqueños generally only admit to the former; and it is near two of the greatest archaeological sites in all Mexico, Monte Albán, and Mitla.'

I shifted around, trying to get comfortable . . .

'Born in 1806, Benito Juárez was the shepherd son of non-Spanish speaking Zapotec Indians, a boy who was taken in hand and educated for the clergy by a local priest, but who, having lost his faith, proceeded to become a lawyer, governor of the state, Chief Justice of the Supreme Court, and finally, in 1858, President of the Republic. He it was who after the fifty or more years of turmoil following Hidalgo and Allende's rising against Spanish rule – years characterized by a war with those Spanish rulers until independence was achieved in 1821, by a war with the United States which resulted in the loss of almost half of Mexico's territory, by financial crises, civil war, and by invasion by England, Spain and France and the setting up by Napoleon III of his puppet monarch Maximilian, the emperor of Austria's younger brother, and the man destined to be shot on the orders of Juárez – he it was who restored, or gave, some measure of unity to the country. This he achieved largely by rallying the different factions of Mexican political life behind him in his fight against Maximilian, but also by confiscating the property of the church, which until the middle of the nineteenth century was the largest landowner in Mexico, and of the other large corporations, including a number of Indian communities.

That this expropriation led, with Juárez's tacit approval, to acquisition of the confiscated land-holdings by private individuals – which in turn led, fairly directly, to the Revolution of 1910 – is, on the whole, as forgotten as that other fact: that Oaxaca was the birthplace of Porfirio Díaz. Who succeeded to the presidency in 1880, ruled as dictator for thirty-one years, and by encouraging unrestricted foreign investment, and enriching still further the rich, ensured that the seeds of revolt which Juárez had planted would flower . . .'

It was tempting, I thought, as I put down my book, turned off the dim little light above my head, and listened to the sound of fifteen other people breathing, sleeping, or lying awake listening to other people breathing and sleeping, to think that history has been so selective in its view of these two sons of Oaxaca because Juárez defeated Maximilian and thus saved Mexico from foreign

domination, and because he was, officially, on the side of freedom, justice and 'the people'. While Díaz, his former protegé,
was on the side of the wealthy, and of European and North-
American capital. But though his victory over Napoleon's puppet
and his liberal stance were undoubtedly factors in the esteem in
which he came to be held – and though Díaz himself was of
largely Mixtec blood – it is difficult not to believe that what really
ensured Juárez's popularity was the fact that he was a Zapotec –
and therefore Mexico's 'First Indian President', as history books
generally define him – and the fact that he adopted an anti-clerical
stance.

For exhausted by wars, no longer really believing in the slogans
shouted at them by politicians, and never perhaps entirely sat-
isfied, despite the gold and blood-spattered statues and the wild
exuberance of their churches, by a religion that was not in the
final analysis *their* religion, the predominantly Indian Mexicans
found in Juarez a link to a 'truer', if not necessarily better, past. A
past in which, as Indians, they had their own cultures and could
feel that those cultures had some relevance in the world. And a
past in which, feeling that their cultures had some relevance in
the world, they could feel that *they* had some relevance in the
world.

Juárez, I told myself as I fell asleep, who while certainly not
uncivilized was equally certainly not European, and, who while
he hadn't readopted the old gods had had the courage to abandon
the new, had proved that one could be Mexican, and exist . . .

*

For all the attendant's warnings – and for all our creaking pace
through the suburbs of Mexico City – when I woke early next
morning the train seemed to be making good progress. And
when I slipped out of my bunk, checked that my wallet was still
with me, and made my way through the still mostly sleeping train
to the observation platform at the rear, I saw that those suburbs
had been replaced by mountains; and the darkness of the night
before by an exhilaratingly blue sky. The trees had huge scarlet
flowers on them; men on donkeys resumed their rightful places
between the rails as soon as we had passed; and children waved
at us with the air of innocents who had never seen a train.

So much for relevance or irrelevance, I thought, as I looked at the scene. With flowers like that, with a sky like that – what does one care about truth?

A question, I suspect, that had occurred to my companions on the observation platform; a very tall other-worldly silver-blonde young American, and his four other-worldly silver-blonde children.

They were staring back down the track as if we were leaving a trail of corruption behind us.

We arrived in Oaxaca, clanking down the main street, at precisely eight-thirty; the time we were due to arrive.

'You see,' the sleeping car attendant said mournfully, and with an absolutely straight face. 'I told you.'

And having taken a taxi to a hotel, and noted, for my part, that the city at first sight was just as attractive as I'd been told it was – a grave dignified place of two-storey colonial houses ('They can't build any higher here, it's very earthquake prone') and, from the faces and costumes to be seen, an almost exclusively Indian population – we proceeded to do all that a visitor to Oaxaca normally does. (After, if that visitor is a nervous Englishman, checking that the walls of the hotel, a converted monastery, are massive enough to withstand the severest earthquake.) We went to the market and ate tamales and drank hot chocolate with cinnamon; we took a bus up to the ruins at Monte Albán; and, though not till the day after, we took a taxi out to the remains at Mitla.

Yet it was not the great ceremonial site at the former, high on a flat hill-top over-looking the city – a site so grand in scale and so magnificent in its setting that it made one feel slightly dizzy – nor the more ornate, down to earth buildings at the latter, with their intricate inlaid brickwork and their old Indian women sitting knitting sweaters in the shadows – in shadows that were almost concrete, so bright was the light – that remained in my memory after I had left Oaxaca. Nor even the fact that my first impression of the city being almost exclusively Indian was confirmed by better acquaintance with it; so much so that one got the idea that, the style of architecture and the somehow incidental point that the churches bore names of Christian saints apart, it was very much as it would have been if the Spaniards had never invaded. (And so much so that one was tempted to think how much better if the Spanish *hadn't* invaded. But seeing those grave dark people

going about their business, wondering, here too, at the abund-
ance of fruit and flowers in the market, and hearing those
different languages, it was difficult not to. And when one became
aware of an atmosphere that one told oneself was unWestern in
its calmness and dignity, and remembered those extraordinary ruins on the hill above, the temptation became almost
irresistible.)

Rather, what stayed with me from Oaxaca was just a little
incident that had nothing to do with history and nothing, really,
to do with the city. A little incident that was both faintly tawdry I
felt, and faintly comic. And a little incident that, though it did,
ostensibly, have nothing to do with the city in which it took place,
did, possibly, have something to do with Mexico, and, again, the
dangers of Mexico.

We were tired after the end of our first day's sight-seeing and
after the previous night spent on the train. So, while we discussed the idea of going to have dinner in a restaurant, we ended
up deciding to have it in the hotel.

At the table next to us there sat a couple in their mid-thirties.
Unlike most of the other guests, who were wearing cotton shirts
and trousers, or cotton skirts, these two were more formally
dressed: he in a black suit with a white shirt and dark tie, she in a
blue suit that a businesswoman might have worn, and a high-
necked, ruffled blouse. Their faces, too, did not look like your
average tourist face; nor did they act like tourists. The man was
thin and had slicked back dark hair and a pale drawn face; and the
woman, only slightly plumper than her companion, had small
blue eyes, crinkly yellowish yet somehow colourless hair scraped
to the back of her head with tortoiseshell combs, and a pale,
nervous mouth. They laughed a lot, and they were constantly
leaning forward and whispering to one another. But they
appeared tense, and ill-at-ease, and even as they laughed his dark
eyes and her blue eyes were darting round the room, as if they
were lizards on the look-out for flies.

They were out of place in this beflowered, thick-walled ex-
convent, and a little disturbing; and I, of course, was intrigued. I
leaned towards them, trying to catch what they were saying or at
least what language they were saying it in. Looking at his thin
white fingers and her redder, fatter hands, I tried to imagine what
they did for a living, and what had brought them here. And

watching their tense laughing mouths as they whispered to one another, as they glanced around and sniggered, as words of scorn, I was practically sure, passed between them about every-thing and everyone in the dining-room, I couldn't help indulging in fantasies, and wondering if they had fangs; or if the tongues with which they wetted their nervous lips were forked.

'Germans,' I mouthed to Patty, who frowned, raised her eyebrows, and mouthed more distinctly 'Germans?'

I nodded.

Patty leaned towards Enrique and passed the message on. Enrique who was small and dark and not at all timid, smiled and said – aloud – 'I know.'

Then, turning to the couple, he asked, in English, if he might borrow their salt, and, almost in the same breath, if they were Germans.

The eyes settled, as if they had spotted their prey; the tongues quickly dampened the lips.

'Yes,' they both said, smiling more broadly than the question or the answer warranted. 'Yes, we are.' And where, they went on, are *you* from?

'My cousin and I are Mexican,' Enrique said. 'And he,' pointing at me, 'is English.'

The eyes flickered now, either in greeting or because this information was, for some reason, amusing.

But there was no word of greeting, from either.

'Are you here on holiday?' Enrique asked.

'Yes, yes,' they both said. 'On holiday.'

'And are you enjoying yourselves?'

Glances were exchanged now between husband and wife (or whatever) as if to say 'What move should we make?' or 'Shall we tell the truth?'

The man smiled and fingered his wedding ring, and then leaned forwards towards Enrique and Patty, purposely excluding me from the conversation.

'No,' he said. 'Not much.' And then, as if it were the sweetest compliment he was paying – and in a pre-echo of what Georgina's homosexuals would say four years later – he added 'We *hate* Mexicans.'

Not for nothing had Enrique studied psychology. He didn't so much as blink. (I didn't see Patty's reaction.)

'Yes,' he said. 'Why?'

The couple appeared delighted; and now it was the woman's turn to speak. Her English wasn't as good as her husband's.

'They are dishonest,' she said. 'They are dirty. They are liars. And,' she said crossly, as if this were the worst of their sins, 'they are *ugly*.'

'Yes,' the man said, no trace of good humour on his face now. 'Yes. They are corrupt. They are unfriendly. And they are stupid. Everything here –' he looked around – 'it is no good. I'm sorry,' he said, quite unapologetically, 'I'm sorry. But that is how it is. I don't think we will be coming back to Mexico. At least,' he added, smiling once again, as if all this had simply been a joke, 'not for a long time.' He glanced at Patty and me, and then looked back at Enrique. 'I'm sorry, he repeated. 'But you did ask, you know.'

At that stage our waiter brought us some coffee, and the couple ordered dessert and started talking to each other again – and laughing – in German. So from then on, to the end of the meal, there was no more contact between the tables; and I assumed, given what had gone on before, that there wouldn't be any thereafter. Just, perhaps, a chilly goodnight from Patty and me, and a more enthusiastic farewell from the determined-not-to-be-put-out Enrique. And after that a discussion about them as we sat in the gardens playing cards, with indignation from the professor, explanation from the psychologist, and fantasy from the writer.

I was, however, wrong. Because as we got up and prepared to sweep off – and after Patty and I had indeed given our chilly nods and Enrique his lofty dear-children-I'm-used-to-such-aggression beam, the couple, with just a quick glance at one another now, beckoned Enrique back. That is to say the man did, while the woman looked on hopefully. And then, half-standing, with his tongue wetting his lips, and watching us watching him, the man whispered into Enrique's ear.

Still Enrique's expression didn't change, though he shook his head.

The man went on, and Enrique shook his head again.

'No,' we saw him say.

The man made one final attempt. He leaned, more lizard-like than ever, right into Enrique's ear, and spoke very rapidly and, he clearly hoped, persuasively. But as Patty and I shifted

impatiently from one foot to the other in the middle of the dining room, Enrique said 'No,' again, and then turned to join us.
'Goodnight,' the couple waved, smiling at us all now as if we had
spent a friendly evening together. 'Goodnight, goodnight, sleep
well.'

'And what,' I said to Enrique as we went into the courtyard
round which the dining-room was built, 'was all that about?'

Enrique smiled, and didn't reply.

'Yes,' Patty said. 'What did they want?'

Again Enrique smiled, and led us over to a candle-lit table. He
shrugged.

'They wanted to go to bed with me, that's all.'

'The two of them?' Patty almost screeched.

'Yes.'

'But – but – they were – they were revolting. I mean – how
horrible.'

'Why?'

'Well they – they . . .' Patty, as she shuddered, became
speechless.

'They weren't very pleasant,' I suggested.

'Oh they were doing that on purpose,' Enrique explained.

'What, all that about how much they hated Mexico? Or rather
hated the Mexicans?'

'Yes. Of course.'

'They meant it.'

'I know, but . . .'

'Well,' I said, 'I'm quite shocked.'

'*Why?*' Enrique insisted.

'Because they were so unpleasant. They were like a couple of
snakes.'

Enrique shrugged.

'And all – their faces – their hands . . .' I started to sputter
myself. 'Oh, I don't know. There was just something obscene
about them. I mean – not as if they wanted to have sex, but as if
they wanted, I don't know, to *humiliate* you. They were all cold
and joyless and – they were just nasty. Unpleasant. That's all.'

'Well I think you're being very prudish,' Enrique purred.

'In that case,' Patty snapped, 'why didn't you go with them?'

'I didn't like them,' Enrique teased her. 'I don't like that sort of
thing.'

'Well then.'

'But I'm not shocked. It's the most normal thing in the world. It happens all the time.'

'Not to me it doesn't.'

'So who's going to get the cards?', Enrique said, as Patty continued to wrinkle her nose and look disgusted.

'I will,' I said, and did; to find Patty still visibly upset when I returned.

As she continued to be for another ten minutes or so, as we sat in the candle light slapping mosquitoes and playing poker.

'Brrr,' she kept on saying. 'Brrr.'

And I too couldn't get rid of the feeling that there had been something evil about that couple, and something tainted about their behaviour and their final suggestion to Enrique. Such coldness didn't belong here, I felt. Such coldness belonged – elsewhere. Not here – amidst the flowers.

'But you know what's really upsetting about it, don't you?' I said at last to Patty, as she began to calm down, and put the Germans out of her mind. 'I mean, really, when you think about it.'

'What?'

'Well – obviously we didn't like them, and of course we would have said no. But frankly – hell – they might have asked us too. I mean – when you come down to it – that's what's *really* insulting . . .'

*

From Oaxaca we took a bus through the night (to avoid the heat Enrique told me at the time; so I wouldn't see the three or four thousand foot drops and the hair pin bends, he told me after) to Tuxtla Guttierrez – a modern rather characterless, though quite agreeable city. From there we hired a car and drove to San Cristóbal de las Casas which was cold, being high in the mountains, and again had a predominantly Indian population. And from San Cristóbel we went on to Montebello, on the Guatemalan border, where there was a National Park dotted with lakes each reputed to be of a different colour, but which all seemed to be, on the day we were there, of a standard lake colour – bluish-green or greenish-blue. Yet despite our travelling so far – driving back to Tuxtla after Montebello, chartering a tiny plane to fly us to the

ruins at Palenque, and then taking a bus to Campeche and
Mérida – and despite our seeing many beautiful sights, it was not
what we saw on this second stage of our journey, any more than
it had been in Oaxaca, that stayed in my memory afterwards. Nor
even any comic-tawdry evidence of the moral dangers of dining
in Mexican hotels. Instead, it was an hour and a half that, it
seemed to me at the time, was likely to be the last hour and a
half of my life; and then it was an experience that was – in retrospect – simply funny.

The first of these memorable occasions took place on, or
consisted of, the home-made plane we chartered, for a nominal
fee, to take us to see the Maya remains at Palenque. (We had tried
to get seats on the regular six-seater plane that flew from Tuxtla to
Palenque every morning – 'around five or six, but you'd better be
here at five; we have to leave before the heat gets up' – but it was
full.) To begin with, as we sat in the tiny old aircraft, with its tiny
old pilot sitting on three telephone directories so he could see out
of the window, I forced myself to be calm, and told myself that at
least this way I would get a wonderful view of the jungle and
mountains that lay between Tuxtla and Palenque. And even my
seeing that according to the fuel gauges we had no fuel didn't
worry me too much. They must just be broken, I shrugged
mentally. Or at least – there must be enough in the tank to last the
forty-five minutes that the flight is supposed to take. I mean –
they couldn't simply have forgotten to fill the thing up before we
left, could they?

No, of course they couldn't, I assured myself as the little thing
bowled down the runway and then, for no particular reason and
with not much conviction, rose into the air.

Of course they couldn't . . .

There was a range of mountains at the end of the runway, but
we cleared that by some fifteen feet; and by the time we had
launched ourselves off the precipice on the other side of it, into a
space that was only sky above and jungle below, for as far as the
eye could see, I was feeling positively blasé. 'Nothing to it old
chap . . .' As in fact I continued to feel for the next twenty
minutes. All right, they probably had forgotten to fill the tanks,
and this plane was only a flying lawn-mower, but – so what? As
long as one has faith –

When we flew over the third of the mountain ranges before

Palenque, we suddenly found ourselves in the middle of a dense, greyish-white fog.

That was when panic took over.

That we had no fuel was bad enough. But that we had no radio, and as far as I could see no compass – indeed, no instruments of any kind that seemed to be working – was likely, I was convinced, to prove fatal. What was more, and what compounded my panic, our little old pilot appeared to think so to. His hitherto express-ionless Indian face started to crease; he started to bite his lips; and he twisted the plane this way and that as he looked for a gap in the fog, and a way out of our predicament. To Patty he said, as if to reassure her, 'I was following the river, but now I can't see the river.'

In other words, I said to Patty, 'We're lost.'

And there were mountains in this fog, and we were flying round in circles, and we had no way of knowing whether we were going up or down, and we had no fuel, and this flight that was only meant to take forty-five minutes had already taken forty and – Oh God, I thought, perhaps it would be quicker and less painful in the long run just to open the door, and jump.

And indeed, though without actually meaning to jump, I realized I had my hand on the flimsy little handle of the flimsy little door . . .

Enrique was silent, and kept looking straight ahead; and the pilot turned to me and gave me a thumbs up sign. But it was to reassure himself, not me.

Meanwhile forty minutes had turned into fifty, and fifty into an hour. Round and round we flew. Up and down we flew. And the fog, it seemed, was getting thicker and thicker, and though it was cold, the sweat was running down my face as I tore at my finger nails and bit the edges of them until I bled. Perhaps if I really hurt myself, I told myself, the crash, when it comes, will hurt less. Or, if I survive, the being torn to pieces by all the animals who live in the jungle below who will fall upon me as I lie trapped in the wreckage; or as I try to pull myself, crippled and wounded, through the undergrowth . . .

Patty alone stayed calm. Sitting up front next to the pilot, she beamed out of the windows, she checked her unbitten finger nails, and – as if nothing out of the ordinary were going on – she even chatted.

'Doesn't she *know*?' I asked myself. 'Doesn't she *realize*?'

'I love flying,' she said to me, turning round without so much as holding anything. 'I always wanted to be a pilot myself.'

She's doing this for show, I thought. She's putting on an act.

'But the possibilities for women pilots are so limited here that I decided it'd be better not to. Though maybe it's not only here.'

I don't believe this, I told myself. She can't be *so* unaware.

'Why?' I managed to stammer, thinking that she might be right to play this game, 'I mean – why do you love flying?'

'I just do. My father was a pilot. He used to take me up with him when I was a girl.'

'Who was he a pilot with?' I said as our pilot flicked the plane on to its side, and then flicked it back again.

(I'm going to throw up. I can't stand it.)

'With the Mexican Air Force to begin with. And then he had a crop-spraying company.'

'And –' Oh God please, please stop this – 'now – is he still a pilot.'

'No,' Patty said, shaking her head. 'He's dead.'

The plane fell in an air-pocket and I thought: That's it. I put my hand over my mouth. But still I forced myself to speak.

'He must have been quite young when he died.'

'Yes,' Patty said. 'He was.'

'What,' I said, determined to keep the conversation light, 'did he die of. Cancer?'

'No,' Patty said, 'he was killed in a plane crash.'

She said it in such a matter-of-fact way that for a moment I saw no connection between her statement and our predicament. Then, when I did, I couldn't help smiling.

'And you tell me now,' I said. 'When we're –'

'Oh this is quite safe,' Patty laughed. 'It's only crop-spraying planes that are dangerous. But this – there's nothing to worry about here. Just as soon as we find a gap in the clouds – don't worry. It's perfectly safe.'

Safe, I wanted to shout. *Safe?*

Almost infuriatingly, Patty was right. Ten minutes later we did find a gap in 'the clouds', as she put it. Then we flew down almost to tree-top level, found the river we'd been navigating by, and followed it till we reached the field at Palenque that served as an airport. (A field in which, unlikely as it was, a taxi was waiting to take us into town.) But though she was right, I made two vows when I got, weak-kneed, into the cab; vows which, I swore, I would keep until I died. One was that I would never again charter a plane, however little it cost or however bad the alternative transport. And the other was that if, in spite of my determination not to, I *did* one day charter another plane, I would always take – or want to take – Patty with me as a fellow passenger.

'He was killed in a plane crash' indeed.

I don't think, under the circumstances, anything else in the world could have made me smile.

The second incident that remained in my mind also took place in Palenque. And if the first concerned our arrival, the second concerned our departure.

We had been in the town three days; the second of which I had spent in bed, being violently sick either as a result of something I had eaten or drunk, or, as I thought more likely, as a delayed reaction to my experiences in the plane. On the afternoon of the third day I nevertheless accompanied Enrique and Patty to the local bus station – a straw-roofed hut in the middle of a patch of wasteland – to buy a ticket on the next bus out; which left, we had been told by the hotel, at six o'clock that evening.

'I have had quite enough of this place,' I told Enrique when he advised me to stay in bed until it was time for our departure.

The ticket office, the hotel had also told us, and an old man sitting on a bench under the only tree in the wasteland had confirmed, was due to open at two-thirty. But at three no one had come, and at three-thirty and four still no one had come. Enrique was getting angry, and even the normally unflappable Patty was beginning to get irritated.

'What will these people think of us?' Enrique asked, indicating the mostly foreign tourists who were wandering around outside the hut. And 'This sort of thing doesn't happen in the north,' Patty murmured.

At four-thirty, however, the ticket office was opened; and when one saw by whom, it almost made the wait worth while. (For me it did, anyway.) Also, even if it didn't make the wait worthwhile, one could see how those last two hours had been spent.

The ticket-seller was tall and very pale skinned with jet-black hair piled high on her head, and a low cut purple satin dress with flounces round the hem. And she maintained the pallor of her skin by protecting herself from the sun, as she stepped in her high-heeled purple satin shoes across the muddy wasteland, with a purple satin parasol.

None of the locals seemed to find this vision extraordinary; obviously they were used to it. All the foreign tourists stared, and an American boy let out a whistle that was more of amazement than admiration. ('Good God,' I said to an ageing hippy who had just asked me if I knew what time the office was opening, and then asked me if I had tried the mushrooms round here. 'Mushrooms?' I had said, mystified and made dense either by my sickness or the wait. 'No. Why? Are they good? I'll ask for some in the hotel restaurant tonight if we don't leave.' The hippy was still staring at *me* with a look of amazement when the ticket-seller turned up.) But Patty and Enrique – Enrique in particular – were merely further put out.

'We've been waiting all this time for this *clown* to put her costume on!'

An attitude that I suspected was likely to cause trouble; and an attitude that, once the ticket-seller had graciously unlocked the hut, installed herself behind a grille, and, having fanned herself a couple of times with a large painted fan, sorted out her tickets, counted her change (with pale scarlet-tipped fingers) and, with the haughtiness of a monarch indicated that we could, if we wished, approach her, certainly did cause trouble. Because by now Enrique and Patty were beside themselves; and while I stood back in the shadows, and the princess gazed through her grille in disdain, Enrique, who was first in line, stepped forward and told her what he thought of her.

Senorita, he began, did she know what time it was? Did she realize she had been keeping all these good people waiting? Did she realize she was a public servant, and not someone who was here to do us a favour?

People like her, he went on, warming to his subject, were what gave Mexico a bad name. People like her were the reason why things didn't work in this country. People like her – people like her – people like her, he finally got out, were the reason why Palenque, apart from its ruins, was such a depressing, shabby *slum*. And now would she, he concluded, his voice shrill by this time kindly, stop fanning herself, stop looking at her finger-nails,

and please sell us three tickets on the six o'clock bus to Mérida.
Please.

'Gracias.'

The purple satin doll didn't even blink. Nor did she stop
making minute adjustments to her nails. She simply looked at
Enrique as if he were the least of God's creatures – and boy did
she know the least when she saw it – said 'No, it's full,' and
turned, with raised and perfectly drawn eyebrows to the person
standing behind Enrique, and snapped 'Next.'

I have to live in this place, her whole manner proclaimed. So I
know what it's like to be stranded here. And if you want to leave
young man, that is not the way to talk to me. Otherwise you'll
find yourself staying here forever. Unless of course you have the
money to hire a car, or you catch the train when and if it passes, or
unless you want to fly back whence you came. But if not – see if
you can get out of here without me. For all I care you *can* stay here
forever. Then you'd know too how it is to rot, and to suffer, and to
grow odd. You'd know too what it's like – to be a civilized
sensitive young white woman; stranded amidst these *Indians* . . .

Enrique became apoplectic, and insisted that the bus to Mérida
wasn't, couldn't be full. But not one more glance did the princess
give him, not one more word did she address to him. And she
was protected by her grille. And so, after thirty seconds of useless
shouting, we were forced to leave, and return to the hotel room
we had vacated at two, when we had walked down to the bus
station with our cases.

'Tomorrow,' I told Enrique, '*I*'ll go and buy the tickets. And
you and Patty stay out of sight.'

They did; and the young woman, though haughty as ever,
didn't even check her list to see if there was room on the bus.

Yes, she said. When do you want to leave?

This afternoon.

So do I, the pale red-tipped hand seemed to say as it pushed
three tickets under the grille. So, oh so do I. But I'm not going to.
Therefore . . .

'Next!'

*

It was in Mérida that Patty left us. And though Enrique and I were
to continue our journey – and I was looking forward to the

remainder of it – and though Patty and I assured one another that we would meet again soon, we both – we all three – felt slightly sad as we said goodbye, since we didn't really believe that we would. For Patty had no plans for coming to Europe, and I had no plans for returning here once I had left.

'You never know,' I smiled. 'Perhaps I'll be commissioned to write a book about Mexico!'

But it didn't seem likely; and as I waved to Patty at Mérida airport, despite the fact that Enrique and I *were* continuing our journey, I had the feeling that I had come to the end of a chapter; or was even closing a book that I had been looking at. A highly coloured picture book perhaps. Or an atlas, open at a part of the world I would never see again.

SEVEN

On Art And Artists (I)

Likely or not, I had come back to Mexico. And now, four years later, I was meeting Patty for lunch. For lunch and, we had agreed over the 'phone, to look at some paintings.

'If you're going to write a book about Mexico,' Patty said, 'you must say something about the muralistas.'

'But I don't like them,' I told her. 'I think they're dreadful.'

'*All* of them?'

'Well, Rivera, Orozco and Siquieros, yes. And if there are others – I'm sure they're no better.'

'But have you seen much of their work?'

'Some. Enough. So I really don't think there's any point in seeing any more.'

'Well I think you should,' Patty insisted. 'At least let's go to the Palacio Nacional and look at the Riveras. And if, after that, you don't like them –'

'If after that I don't like them,' I said, 'I'm giving up on them forever.'

'All right,' Patty said. 'That's a deal. But at least – *look*.'

So, after we had eaten, we did.

Rivera, it is generally held, was the foremost of the three painters who, children of the 1910 Revolution, sought to become, and in a sense became, the first truly Mexican artists. Certainly their work has dominated Mexican art this century; and certainly their vision of Mexico is to a great extent the vision that the world – via Hollywood – has of Mexico. And yet this very dominance, this very role of interpreter that they both sought and had thrust upon them, has something to do with the fact that despite their greatness – for they are, too, great painters, which only makes matters worse – they are, in my opinion, bad artists. It also has something to do with the fact that after I had taken the Metro to the Zocalo with Patty, walked across the huge square, and gone into the Palacio Nacional – and after we had climbed the stairs to the first floor balcony and looked at the series of murals illustrating the history of Mexico that Rivera had painted on the walls – I still couldn't change that opinion. For though their draughtsmanship and colouring were skilled, and though they possessed the originality, the uniqueness that proclaims that the man who painted these was great, they also proclaimed that the vision Rivera had of Mexico – and that he then presented to the world – was flawed. Not just because – as one could see from the pastiche Indian style, the conscious 'understandability' – it was a crude, simplistic, ultimately patronizing and sentimental vision – as if the artist considered that 'the people' were only capable of understanding that which was crude and deliberately simple – but also because the mind that conceived that vision, and therefore the hand that gave it expression, was dishonest. Dishonest in its determination to see the world and its inhabitants as flat, one-dimensional, and there again 'simple' things, and dishonest in its attitude to painting – to art – itself. And that, perhaps, was the crux of the matter.

'At any rate,' I said to Patty, wagging my finger at her, smiling, but nevertheless serious, 'it seems to me that that is the crux of the problem. You see . . .'

And then I launched into one of my favourite theories.

Artists, I started, and by artists I mean painters, writers, actors, dancers, singers, sculptors and anyone else who can make a claim to creativity, are the buffoons of this world; the Rigolettos, if you like, of the Dukes of Mantua. Their role and purpose in life is to amuse the Duke, to entertain the Duke, and to stand on their heads and perform somersaults when the Duke, or any of his courtiers, wants them to. In return for this service they are granted perhaps a little more freedom than is normally permitted to the Duke's subjects, a certain amount – or a great deal, if they perform well and are lucky – of fame and fortune, and above all, the liberty to believe that they are not the Duke's creatures. Yes, as long as you dance, as long as you sing – and never mind the tune; for the Duke and his courtiers have varied tastes, and they even at times like songs that criticize the court – you can fool yourself that however much you compromise yourself at court, your integrity, like a virginal daughter, is safely locked up at home. You can also fool yourself that you are not in fact the Duke's creature at all, and that you truly are a free spirit, whose purpose, duty and destiny in life it is, far from amusing or entertaining the Duke, to tweak, if do nothing more radical, the Duke's beard.

Poor fools.

For though it is possible for the very great, for the genuinely great to tweak the Duke's beard – tweak it, generally, even as the Duke thinks it is being stroked, or even as he thinks it is all being done in jest – for most artists no such freedom exists. All they can do is play the part that history, genetics, or their up-bringing has prepared them for, and, even while believing they are doing the opposite – even, often, while appearing to the world to do the opposite – stroke what they most would tweak.

Of course some – most – artists are quite happy to stroke. (The tweaking of the really great may be, indeed, involuntary.) Others would like to tweak, know that ultimately they cannot, and either transfer their allegiance to another Duke, in the normally vain hope that he will be better than his brother, or use their knowledge to give their work more depth and more resonance. But others, a few, are determined to take seriously that most important of all privileges that the Duke grants them, and believe that they are genuinely uncompromised, and genuinely free to tweak.

These are the dishonest ones, the ones you had better watch. (For as long as no one tries to take away that most important of privileges, they will support the most ruthless, the most tyrannical of Dukes. They, to preserve the illusion that they are not in the service of murderers, will close their eyes, or, like Siquieros, who tried to assassinate Trotsky but killed someone else instead, will even take part in a murder.) And these, I concluded, wagging my finger at Patty again, still smiling but still quite serious, are the Riveras of this world.

'I mean,' I said, coming down to earth now, and nodding towards one of the paintings, 'do you actually *like* these things?'

'Well,' Patty said, and hesitated. Then she mumbled something about them being historically important, culturally important for Mexico.

'Yes, I know all about that. But we're not talking about history, are we. Nor about culture. We're talking about paintings. And as paintings – tell me honestly – do you like them?'

Patty frowned, and then laughed. 'No,' she said. 'I don't.'

'You see,' I crowed. 'You see. And what is more, I've never actually met anyone in my life who liked them. I've met people who admire them, and I've met people who say "Well you've got to understand them, see them in their context". But actually to like them – I don't see how anyone could.'

(Though no doubt there are many people who do.)

'I mean,' I continued, trying to underline my point, 'they might appeal to intellectuals. To people who don't really like paintings. As people who don't really like opera tend to say that *Fidelio* is their favourite opera. But to the people who they were presumably meant to please, to so-called ordinary people – no, no, and no. Apart from anything else,' I started to switch off my motors, feeling I had gone on long enough, 'he makes the people he paints – the people he is supposed to be painting for – look so ugly. He despises them even as he paints them. Oh, he thinks he's being honest, but – nobody's that ugly. Nobody *real* is that ugly. Only people in the eye of someone who feels contempt for them. Only people –' and my mind went back to the German tourists in Oaxaca, as I finally came to an end, 'who are really ugly themselves.'

'Oh I don't know,' Patty laughed, taking one last look at a painting of an Indian on his knees offering a gift to a white man. 'I think they're fairly accurate. All right – maybe they're not that bad. But –' she wrinkled her nose, and laughed again, 'I think, on the whole – the Mexicans *are* rather ugly.'

*

It was a word I was to hear again and again before I left Mexico, from Mexicans and foreigners alike.

'Because they're *ugly*,' Georgina said unhesitatingly, when I asked her why she felt, as she claimed to, so out of place in Indian Mexico.

'Because they *are* ugly,' Eugenia – who hasn't yet come into this story, but will – laughed; when I asked her why, in her opinion, the Indians, with one or two principally Olmec exceptions, were always represented in pre-Columbian sculpture – as they were by the muralistas – in such an unflattering – such a wilfully unflattering, such a falsely unflattering – way.

'But above all because they're so *ugly*,' a friend of Eugenia's ended her catalogue of complaints about Mexico, when she was explaining to me why she hadn't been out of her apartment for ten years. 'Ugly, ugly, *ugly*.'

And yet, though I did hear this word so often, and though I myself had noted that pre-Columbian statues of men and women are for the most part hideous, and that the mixture of Indian and Iberian features is not a particularly happy one, I always felt, when I heard it, that I wasn't simply hearing some more or less frivolous aesthetic judgement. Rather I was hearing a sort of nostalgic longing for Europe, that the people who expressed it didn't know how to express in any other way. Not for a real Europe, maybe. But for a Europe of their dreams; for an imaginary, idealized Europe. For a Europe that they had, in a sense, never left; and for a Europe, at least with part of themselves, that they would have liked to return to.

To a continent, their words seemed to echo, where it was – or had been – possible to dream . . .

*

Before I met Eugenia and her friends however, and started to be aware of how often the word ugly cropped up in their conversation, I had to take my trip with Georgina, and to see, as it were, two further chapters in this book getting themselves written. And before I could even set off with Georgina, I had to experience what I could only think of, both at the time and afterwards, as – a touching episode.

EIGHT

A Touching Episode

I was leaving for my trip with Georgina on Monday; when I got back my visit to the 'Indian village' was to be arranged and undertaken. But by the time I did get back, Patty would have returned to the north; and though I said I would like to visit her there – as I had never been to Sonora, or anywhere in the north – I wasn't sure that I would, since I hadn't made any definite plans, and still wasn't sure where I wanted to go, or what I wanted to do. So when she suggested, after I had finished lecturing her about Rivera's shortcomings, that I have lunch with her the following day too – though at Enrique's parents' house – I said yes, of course, and thank you.

'After all, who knows when, or if . . .'

'No,' Patty said. 'You're coming. It's all settled.'

'Yes all right, but just in case – and anyway, I'd like to come tomorrow whether I come to Hermosillo or not.'

It was after lunch however – after an enormous lunch, that started with fruit salad, went on to lasagne, continued with fish, and ended, several courses later, with home-made cakes – and cream – and brandy – and chocolates – and 'you must have some of these cookies or Alicia will be offended: she made them specially for you' – that the touching episode took place.

We were sitting, in the fading light – it was about six-thirty by now – in the living room, sleepy with too much food and drink. We were waiting for Enrique's sister, who had said she would drop by to say hello at six, but who would probably not show up, her father said, until eight. None of us knew quite what to do to fill in the time, and bloated and tired as we all were, we didn't have much desire to talk.

I stroked the dog when it came into the room and jumped up on my chair.

Patty read a travel catalogue.

Mr F adjusted his tie, and sighed, and Mrs F smiled vaguely up towards the ceiling, clasping her knees with her hands.

The light continued to fade; and no one had the energy to stand and turn on a lamp.

Gloomier and gloomier; sleepier and sleepier.

The only noise was from the kitchen; where Alicia, the housekeeper, was washing the dishes.

Clink. Clank. Clink.

Or . . .

It was Mr F who finally broke the silence, and the spell. Getting up, he not only did turn on a lamp, but he asked me, rather mournfully, if I would like to hear a record.

'Look,' he said, 'I have a lot of new ones.'

He leaned over, picked up a pile of albums from the floor, and handed them to me.

They certainly were new, I saw, as I started to flick through them. Most of them were still inside their cellophane wrappings. And even those that had been opened didn't look as if they had been played. Merely prepared in case, one day, anyone should want to listen to them. How peculiar, I thought, as I worked my way through the pile, and looked at the names on the sleeves. How very peculiar.

Pavarotti. Domingo. Sutherland. Carreras . . .

My surprise was not so much caused by these records never having been played; though it did strike me as odd that anyone should have bought so many records merely to look at. More, it was due to the nature of the music, and the performers.

Four years ago Enrique had told me that while his father liked music he hated opera, and couldn't bear to listen to it in any form. (The nearest he ever got to it in my presence was one day when he put on a record of *The King and I* by mistake. He took it off after two minutes saying 'Pah, pah.') Yet now – could it be, I asked myself (ah, vanity, vanity) that knowing I was coming for lunch – though he didn't, presumably, know until last night, when Patty must have told him – and knowing that I liked opera, he had gone out this morning and bought some thirty records? No, of course not, that was absurd. Well then, I thought, could it be that someone had *given* him all these records? But there again, that didn't seem likely; since anyone who knew him well enough to give him thirty records presumably also knew him well enough to be aware of his dislike of opera. Only – if he hadn't bought them for me, and he hadn't been given them, and they hadn't been played – it was a mystery to which I could think of no solution.

'Well,' the elderly distinguished-looking professor asked me, 'what would you like to listen to? Björling? Domingo? Di Stefano? Corelli?'

He knew all the names, anyway.

'I don't know,' I said, thinking maybe I should respect his tastes, and say I didn't want to listen to anything, or would prefer to listen to something orchestral. 'You've got so much.'

On the other hand he seemed eager that I should listen to one of these new records he had handed me; as if he wanted to prove that while he might not like opera himself, the contentment of his guests was of greater importance to him. And knowing that I did . . .

'But,' I said, handing him a record of Joan Sutherland, 'how about this?'

I chose that particular record for two reasons. One was I thought that the sound of a woman singing might disturb the still somewhat sleepy atmosphere – and thus Mr F himself – less than a man; and the other was that while I had never particularly liked Joan Sutherland as a singer myself, I had noticed that on one side of the record she was singing not just operatic arias, but songs by Ivor Novello, Noel Coward, and Richard Rodgers. Maybe, I thought, if Mr F can't stand opera, he will find that sort of music marginally more acceptable, and put side B of the record on.

I settled down to listen.

First of all, Mr F didn't put side B on; he put side A on.

Second, having listened for a moment or two, he nodded, and turned the volume up.

And third, having sat down again, he proceeded to listen to the record with such intensity, such total and almost unbreathing concentration, that he cast another sort of spell on the room, and Patty, Mrs F and I all found ourselves listening with the same degree of intensity as he did. And now not even from the kitchen was there any noise. There was only – in the whole world one felt – Joan Sutherland.

I have never liked her . . .

And yet, sitting in that room, listening to her Norma, her Lucia, her Elvira, her Marguerite – listening to her through the ears, as it were, of Mr F – it was impossible not to like her. It was as if a small boy had suddenly seen a butterfly for the first time; a butterfly one had always dismissed as uninteresting oneself. And yet, being with that boy, one couldn't help seeing the creature with his eyes, and finding it, despite what one had always felt, miraculous. That such a creature should exist . . . Obviously one knew that as soon as the small boy had stopped gazing one would lose that sense of the miraculous, and return to one's old prejudices in favour of red admirals, or swallow tails. But while he did – while he cast that spell and made one see through his eyes – for all that one knew the names of those other butterflies, and knew that one liked them more, for the moment they didn't exist. For the moment nothing else in the world existed. Just *that* butterfly. Just *that* beauty. Just *that* miracle.

'Listen to her,' Mr F whispered. 'Listen to her. That range. That security. That *purity*.' He looked around, from his wife to his niece to me. 'She's a miracle,' he whispered, and shook his head. 'A miracle.'

When side A was over, and he put side B on – and when Joan Sutherland's enchantment started to fade, and Mrs F picked up her knitting – Mr F turned from the record player and his adjustment of the volume and tone, and went, without a word, upstairs.

So much, I thought, for miracles.

For half an hour, yes – and then he has to leave the room.

But I was wrong; for a minute later he returned, and for the next hour and a half, until his daughter arrived, he sat and listened quite happily to the rest of the Sutherland record, and then to Domingo and Pavarotti. Even if he never again seemed quite so enraptured as he had before, nor made us hear the singers through his ears.

While I was listening I flicked through a browning, flaking magazine, which was what Mr F had gone upstairs to fetch.

On the cover there was a sepia photograph of some French land-girls 'preparing to defend their country.'

The date on the magazine was February, 1940.

'Page twenty-three,' Mr F hissed. 'Page twenty-three.'

On page twenty-three there was a photograph of a dark-haired young man, looking very serious and wearing a suit and a tie. Underneath the photograph was the following caption. 'A recent study of the brilliant young tenor A F, who made his debut at the

Palacio de Bellas Artes last month. A F's performance was greeted by loud cheers and glowing reviews, and a great future is predicted for this excellent artist.'

'The war was on in Europe,' Mr F murmured. 'There was no possibility of going there to continue my studies or my career. And as I already had my degree in engineering, and was already getting interested in astronomy . . .'

NINE

San Miguel de Allende

Guanajuato, everyone had told me and I had read, was a beautiful town, and the place where Hidalgo and Allende's heads had been displayed in public for ten years after their execution by the Spanish. Querétaro was a commercial centre with fine colonial architecture and wide squares; and was where Allende had planned and then raised his flag of revolution in 1810, and where Maximilian was shot, fifty-seven years later. And Dolores Hidalgo was the village that was notable only for its being the place in which Hidalgo had given his call to arms when he learned that the plans he had made with Allende had been discovered and a warrant was out for his arrest; and from which he set out with three hundred people armed with knives and sticks to start a war that would end only eleven years later in independence for Mexico.

I wanted to see all these places – and had decided, with Georgina, that I would see them – both because they were reputed to be beautiful and because they and the whole region of the Bajio had played such an important part in recent Mexican history. But the town I above all wanted to visit, and the town that really decided us in favour of the Bajio – as opposed, say, to a trip to El Tajin and Vera Cruz, and the States to the north and north-east I hadn't yet visited – was another; and one that, perversely, I was certain I would dislike even before I went there.

San Miguel de Allende is about a four hour drive north of Mexico City; and is extolled, in every guide and travel book, as being a 'jewel amongst Mexican cities'. Its position amidst the mountains, its cobbled streets, its carefully preserved colonial architecture, its place in history as the town on which Hidalgo's mob marched after they had left Dolores – all these are cited as reasons why San Miguel is so special, and so worth a visit. 'An exquisite town', 'The loveliest of all towns' one can read; and in fact the whole place has been declared a national monument by the Mexican government, so it can be preserved intact.

More ominously, all those books cite another reason for visiting San Miguel. It is, they say, 'an artists' colony'. And not just any old artists' colony. It is the leading artists' colony in Mexico.

'Dear God,' I said to Georgina: 'can you imagine anything more grim?'

I was half-joking when I said this; but the reality was grim indeed . . .

Already, before we left Mexico City, I began to think that what I had said in semi-jest might turn out to be true. For though we were due to leave at eight in the morning – thereby avoiding the heat of the day – we didn't in fact leave till twelve, thereby getting the worst of it. The delay wasn't really Georgina's fault – she had to see someone 'briefly' before we left, and briefly turned out to be for three hours – but because of this, because neither of us had slept enough the night before (having got up at six in order to make our early start), and because we were both still liable to slip back into the antagonism of four years before, we became, although we were very consciously on our best behaviour, slightly tetchy. A tetchiness that revealed itself, on my part, as a feeling of tightness round the eyes and a certain thinning of the lips; and on both our parts as a still greater tendency to be friendly thoughtful and polite.

The effort made us even tetchier . . .

'Are you sure there's not too much wind?'

'Are you sure you wouldn't like to eat something before we leave?'

'Are you sure you really want to go?'

And that was just the start.

Things did not improve much once we were on the road. To begin with, the traffic was very heavy, and having nearly crashed changing lanes on the motorway out of town we had to wait for half an hour just to get the tank filled. (And also got overcharged for some oil we bought. 'Never mind,' I snapped, when Georgina threatened to make a scene. 'It's not worth fighting about.' And then, feeling my lips getting thinner, I smiled. 'Never mind,' I repeated. 'It's still only half what you'd pay in England.' 'That,' Georgina snarled, 'is hardly the point.' Then she too remembered what she had to do, and beamed. 'Oh well,' she tossed away lightly into the fume-filled air. 'What the hell.')

After that I discovered, though she had said before that she was not, that Georgina was a fast driver, and she discovered – though I had told her before that I was – that I was a nervous passenger.

'I'm not going *too* fast am I?' she said – she smiled – as we zipped along in her little Renault that, when we went over one hundred and twenty kilometres an hour, started to shudder and shake.

'No, no,' I said – I smiled – two seconds before stamping down both my feet onto imaginary brakes, as a truck pulled out ahead of us.

'Sorry,' I said, 'instinctive, But I did warn you,' I added – only just managing a smile now – 'I was a nervous passenger.'

'Yes, yes,' Georgina said tightly, and possibly managed to smile again herself. But I wasn't watching her now. I had my eyes on the road ahead. Ready to brake again . . .

And then, while the roads to the south – to Puebla, to Cuernavaca – climbing as they did up through forests, and giving one both the chance to see spectacular views and breathe fresh mountain air, were exhilarating and redolent, somehow, of all that lay beyond, those to the north were in almost every respect the opposite. If they climbed – as they had to, to get over the mountains that surround the seven thousand foot high city on all sides – they climbed not through forests, but through shabby suburbs, through industrial estates, through an interminable splurge of one-storey shacks and un-made up roads, and an atmosphere of dusty desolation. If they gave one a chance to breathe a different air from the city below it wasn't a better air but a still worse air; an air that was yellow with sulphur, grey with diesel fumes, and murky with substances of which it was preferable, one felt, not to know the origins. And finally, if the roads to the south promised ripeness and life, this to the north promised sterility, dryness, and desert.

A promise that, as we drove on under the ever hotter sun, was ever more maintained. Such vegetation as there was looked exhausted. Such colours as there were looked bleached. And such people as were about – people on foot, people on donkeys, people simply sitting by the roadside or outside their houses – looked not purposeful, part-of-the-land, in short, Indian, as the people in the south had looked, but rather disconsolate, displaced, and, in their shabbiness, their obvious poverty, and their sense of being condemned to an existence that was as unyielding

and joyless as the stony cactus-covered mountainsides on which
they lived, quite un-Indian or de-Indianed. They murmured to
one constantly, with their presence, that this was a land no man
was meant to dwell in, or to try to scratch a living from.

A harsh barren road, through a harsh barren land; and a road
that would only end in San Miguel . . .

(Coming back we took this same road, which is, for most of its
way, a four-lane highway to Querétaro. But then, travelling in the
late afternoon and early evening as we were – and not having San
Miguel as our goal – not only the road but the landscape, the
vegetation and the people took on an entirely different aspect.
The mountains remained forbidding, cactus was still almost the
only form of greenery, and it still didn't look as if living in one of
those little faded pastel shacks, up there amidst the stones, could
have been the easiest or most sensual of existences. And yet –
with the light pink and golden on the hillsides, with the pigs and
the chickens scrabbling around in the dirt, and the people suddenly restored, in the setting sun, to some sort of unity with the
land – and looking, themselves, somewhat less implacable than
they had at two-thirty in the afternoon – there was a certain
nobility in the scene. A certain sense of dour rightness that made
one think that if this undoubtedly wasn't the best of all possible
worlds, it very probably, as far as one can judge such things
objectively, wasn't anywhere near the worst.)

But if the journey had started badly and things had not improved as it continued, the final stretch, from Querétaro – which
we decided to see on our return – to San Miguel itself was,
without any question, the most wretched. We were tired; we
were hot; and our effort to be friendly had reduced us both to
silence. (Or to lapidary banalities like: 'How hard life is for most
people, when you think about it.') The countryside was still more
uncharitable than it had been on the highway, with the added
defects of it being quite frighteningly deserted and, this particular
afternoon, not at all improved as the sun got lower in the sky.
And the car, that according to Georgina she had been having
trouble with recently, started to shudder even when we were
going at less than one hundred and twenty; and made me think
that at any moment it would stop, leaving us stranded, so to
speak, on the moon.

'Maybe,' I said to Georgina, 'we should go a bit slower.'

Georgina didn't take her foot off the accelerator.

'The sooner we arrive,' she muttered, 'the better.'

Well that, I thought, as we raced along the high and lonely road, where the only signs of life – or former life – were the corpses of dogs on the asphalt, remains to be seen.

But I didn't say anything, and simply concentrated, as before, on braking, shifting gear when necessary, and willing the unsteady little Renault to stay on the road. Forty-five kilometres, a sign said. And then, what seemed like miles later, forty-four.

Meanwhile, I was certain, up in the hills above us vultures were starting to gather . . .

The streets of San Miguel are cobbled, the guide-books had said; and indeed they are. So cobbled that driving over a rocky beach must have been smoother; and our relief at having survived the lunar drive to the town was lessened almost as much by the suspicion that what wasn't already broken in the car would probably break now, as by the confirmation, practically the moment we arrived, of every one of our doubts about this place; this artists' colony that was a jewel amongst Mexican cities.

Almost.

San Miguel was loathsome. The houses, though some were theoretically 'pretty', did not appear lived in, and therefore looked dreary, and drab. The inhabitants either seemed to be engaged in the tourist-trade or some part of it – waiters, hotel-keepers, soft-drink pedlars, sellers of funny hats and wooden knick-knacks and what-nots and general tack – or, as nowhere else in Mexico, to have taken to the begging trade as if there were a shortage in the industry; and to have chopped off limbs here and there and disfigured themselves as if they aspired to be in some so-called 'Mexican' movie. And the tourists, the 'artists', the frequenters of 'International Schools' – the blonde overweight divorcees in their beige pants, clutching sketching pads under their arms, the no longer quite young would-be Hemingways leaning against the side of their pick-up trucks and jeeps, rubbing their moustaches and drinking beer as they discussed literature, and generally tried to prove, with every solid nod, with every scratch of the belly, that one could be an artist *and* a regular guy – were, to say the least, dispiriting. All these people who had, probably quite unwittingly, created this caricature of a Mexican town; a Hollywood Mexico of dust (for there was a wind here, and the air was filled with dust), of lame dogs, of beggars and cripples and waiters who snarled and smiled as they served you.

To some extent they were dispiriting because they seemed, most of them, ill at ease in their roles. But more, because they looked – and this almost without exception – unhappy. As if they knew that this whole place had been fabricated for them, and by them; and as if they knew that just out there, just over those hills, there was another Mexico, an entirely different Mexico, and a Mexico they would have liked, even loved, if they had gone there. But they were cursed for some reason to stay here; and they didn't have the strength to shake off that curse. The long thin woman sitting in the main square, dragging on a long thin cigarette; one could see that she hated it here. The two fair-haired girls and the two dark-haired boys sitting at a table in a restaurant, looking over their shoulders, flapping at flies, trying in vain to catch the waiter's eye and trying, in vain, to pretend they didn't mind that they couldn't – 'I mean this is Mexico, and you expect bad service' – one could see; they hated it here. And the lean, brown, balding, late middle-aged man in his jeans and plaid shirt, walking along the cobbles with the gait of an athletic youth and the exalted slightly crazed air of one who has decided that the only refuge from negative-thinking is sanctity; one could see – not very far under that jaunty hey-man-no-shit mask – he *hated* it here. Those who were here for a day, those who were here for a month, those who had decided 'to get out of the rat-race' and come down south 'where you can really get in touch with life' and were resident here – they hated it, every one of them; and were unhappy.

The only exceptions one saw were those people who looked as if they had known in advance what San Miguel would be like, and had come here just for that. Come here in their white cars and put up at the best, or the next-to-best hotel; just so they could be waited on by servile, hostile waiters, could brush aside cripples and beggars as they bought souvenirs they didn't want, could look at all those sad unhappy people with artistic pretensions, and aspirations to be regular guys.

Just so they could lie back in the sun by their swimming pools and, as they called for another drink, despise.

Yes, there were one or two of these; who had come down south to satisfy their need for contempt, for a confirmation of their belief that only man, that only *they*, were vile.

'Fucking Mexicans. Goddam Third World . . .'

I will say this for San Miguel however: the prevailing genius of the place did everything in its power to protect us, and keep us from the town. For a start it tried to scare us off by making the approach road so forbidding, and practically causing the car to break down. And then, when we did nevertheless get there, and had parked, started to walk around, and seen how wretched everything and everyone was, it did everything in its power to make us leave again immediately. It made it impossible for us to find a bar, where we could sit and have something to drink. It made it impossible for us, once we had given up the idea of sitting down, to find any drink that was cold, or even cool. (The bottles were all kept in refrigerators on the stalls and in the shops, only none of the refrigerators were plugged into any power supply.) And finally, when we had decided that the only thing to do was check into a hotel and have a shower, it made it impossible for us to find a hotel. (Apart from the first place we tried; which had one tiny room without a window.)

But we, foolishly, were not appreciative of the efforts of the genius of San Miguel, and persisted in our determination to stay. And eventually, after we had walked up and down practically every street in town, and gone into almost every hostelry we could find ('Do you have rooms free?' we asked at one place, and the desk clerk snapped 'No' without looking up. 'Do you have rooms free?' we asked at another; and the woman in the courtyard laughed 'Tomorrow!') – it gave up trying to drive us away, and allowed us to find a room – a big room, with a balcony, with a bathroom! – in the very last hotel we decided to ask at. ('If they haven't got anything there – we're getting out of here. It doesn't matter how tired we are. *Anything's* better than staying in this dump.')

Thank God, we said, as we collapsed into chairs and beds. Thank God.

'Who's going to take a shower first?'

But the genius of San Miguel either wanted to punish us for so ignoring its warnings, or wanted to prove to us that we should have heeded them.

For though it had allowed us to find a hotel room, and a hotel room with a bathroom – it had not allowed us to find a hotel room with any water.

After that – as Georgina screeched 'It's not possible' and marched off downstairs to speak to the management – it left us to our own devices, being neither malevolent nor protective. Probably it had gone off to warn other would-be visitors to San Miguel. To rattle their cars and to whisper 'Don't come, don't come, don't come.'

'We're very sorry,' the woman at the desk apparently told Georgina. 'But there's no water anywhere in San Miguel. That is – there's a chronic shortage. There are so many tourists you see, and it hasn't rained for so long – and the wind blows and the dust gets into your eyes and under your finger-nails – that we never have enough. However,' she apparently added, 'if you try in about half an hour there should be enough for a quick shower. And if you like – I'll charge you half the rate for your room.'

Georgina would have liked – we both would have liked – a lot of water and the full rate. But we accepted the offer; managed, after half an hour, just as the woman had predicted, to squeeze enough water out of the pipes for us both to have a quick – if very cold – shower; and realized that the effect of all these little trials was to make us forget our tetchiness and start to get on well together. As we continued to, with only the occasional argument, for the rest of our travels.

'The best thing about this place,' I told Georgina, as we stood on the balcony looking out over a view of roof-tops and distant mountains that had been improved by our showers and was, at last, being further improved by the light of a setting sun, 'is that tomorrow we'll be leaving it and with luck will never have to see it again.'

'You're not going to say all these things in your book, are you?'

'I certainly am. I shall say that San Miguel de Allende is the ugliest, most depressing, most dispiriting town I have seen in Mexico – and if you're going to Mexico, avoid it.'

'That'll only make anyone who reads it want to go.'

'That's up to them.'

'Anyway, it's not true. I mean it's not that bad.'

'It may not be true,' I said. 'But it *is* that bad. It's a place that seems to have lost all reason for its existence. It's a place that seems to have had its blood sucked out of it. And worst of all – it's a place which all these people here, when they go back home, will think of as being typically Mexican – and will tell all their friends is typically Mexican. "Oh you should see the dirt, the little children with their hands out, and the donkeys. And no water, any-where." And it isn't typically Mexican. It's the least typically Mexican town I've seen. It's a tourist town. It's a so-called artists' town. And artists, as we all know,' (I had explained my theories to Georgina, too) 'are buffoons. And therefore – But oh, enough of San Miguel,' I said. 'Let's think where we're going to have dinner. And when we're having dinner – let's think where we're going to go tomorrow . . .'

*

Dolores Hidalgo was the answer to that. Dolores Hidalgo – and afterwards – Guanajuato.

*

San Miguel has stuck in my mind as a little grey vision of hell; the sort of place one tells oneself one would prefer Siberia to; or the Gobi desert. And not even the possibility that I formed the opinion I did simply because I was tired, had been tense all day, and have a prejudice against 'artists' colonies', makes me want to return. I like to think it was hellish, although I am prepared to admit that were I to return I might well find it charming; or something of the sort. After all, it does seem difficult to believe that my sense, the morning after, that the landscape leaving town was as beautiful and gentle as the landscape entering town was ugly and brutal, didn't have something to do with the fact that I had slept surprisingly well, after having had a surprisingly good dinner. (In a monumental stone-vaulted former monastery res-taurant, where the only other clients were two Americans who, I learned by eavesdropping, had arrived that day and were as unenchanted with the place as we were, and what looked to be the remnants of San Miguel high society. A single family consist-ing of a gloomy, dark-suited father, a mournful, black-laced mother, a dour, silent son, and a ripe, gorgeous, amazingly-coiffed daughter. All of whom looked as if they had been sitting out the decline of their home-town on some nearby hacienda, from which they emerged perhaps once a week to remind the world of the way things had been, and, from the look of three of the four, the way they wished things still were. The daughter alone, perfectly skinned, shining-lipped, on the plump side but flawless, looked as if she were content with the present, and the way things were right at this moment.)

Yet, typically, though I disliked it so much, and though the following morning I did find the road out of town so very different from the road entering town (as did the car, apparently: not another shudder did it give for the next four days), it made a far greater impression on me than Dolores Hidalgo, Guanajuato, Guadalajara, Querétaro, or all the other places we visited, put together.

Dolores, for example, was a small town with low pink and blue and green and white buildings, a church (*the* church, where Hidalgo issued his summons), clean streets and amiable people going about their business – and having, it seemed, some business to go about. Guanajuato, also pink and blue and green and white, was the very opposite of San Miguel, and deserved its reputation as the most beautiful city in Mexico. (With a vaulted subterranean road system, an ornate theatre and large university, it had the air of a well-endowed provincial garden town that had managed to hang onto to the self-confidence which being the centre of the world silver trade up to a hundred years ago gave it.) Guadalajara, the second largest city in the republic, with a population of around five million, had, despite its size, an even more marked self-confident provincial air; the air of a city with a well-established middle-class of mainly Spanish descent keeping its end up, and finding its pleasure in shaded streets, fountained squares, and in concerts, plays, and dance.

(Of course there was a crisis here too, as the shacks and the crime statistics and the people one spoke to proclaimed. And there were problems that hadn't even been faced, let alone overcome. And yet – still Guadalajara held up its skirts to keep them out of the mud, and still one felt it would take a lot more in the way of crises, of unemployment, of poverty, crime and hunger really to make that middle-class stumble, to lose its self-confidence. It would take more than that to stop it believing that for all the problems that beset the city, this was, neverthe-less, the right direction in which to be heading, and the best way of going about things. Not in any high idealistic sense, but in a day-to-day sense. In a sense that prefers the shade of a tree to the shade of a concrete shelter; in a sense that values architecture – the most practical and having-to-be-lived-with art – above even concerts and plays and dance; and in a sense that prizes the flower above all.

In Mexico City the middle-class, though dominant, was only just hanging on, and one could feel its grip slipping minute by minute. But in Guadalajara – Oh, they were *suffering*, of course, and the school fees were rising *horrendously*, but even so – they hadn't even started to slip. And nor, if they could do anything about it, did they intend to. Back into the darkness. Back into chaos. Back into the past . . .)

Irapuato had dust and strawberries everywhere. Celaya was clean and also had strawberries. And Querétaro, at the end, was a smaller, more industrial, somehow tougher and less consciously 'gracious' city than either Guanajuato or Guadalajara, though it too had its share of fountains and pedestrian malls and florid churches. (It was in Querétaro, that the car, which had started to shudder again, finally broke down. But after a week of travelling through often very desolate country where the nearest tele-phone, let alone service station, might have been fifteen, twenty, or even fifty miles away, it did so precisely one hundred yards from the principal, possibly the only Renault concessionary in the whole region. The problem was simple. The fan-belt, that had now broken, had not been the right fan-belt for the car. Indeed, it hadn't been the fan-belt for a car at all. Fitted at a garage near Georgina's apartment in Mexico City, it had been lifted, the mechanic in Querétaro laughed, from a washing machine. 'You see,' he crowed. 'That'll teach you to live in the big city. Come here. Come out to the provinces. There we know the difference between a car and a washing machine. Or at least – we won't try to cheat you quite so often.') But none of these towns, really, could compare with San Miguel. They were simply – some more, some less – beautiful, pleasant, easy towns that for all their uniquely Mexican flavour, had much in common with pleasant, easy towns elsewhere in the world. With Bath or York. With San Francisco or Savannah. With Verona, Bergamo or Florence.

But San Miguel – San Miguel was special. For while there are other towns in the world that seem to exist merely as tourist towns – Venice, for instance, or Vienna – they have, nevertheless, preserved some vitality, some life of their own; a life that could, one imagines, always be nursed back into good health some day. Whereas San Miguel, beyond any hope of recovery, was dead; its blood sucked out by the unhappy vampires who lived in it or visited it. Vampires who needed blood to survive and reproduce; and vampires who, lacking blood (and clearly not actually wanting blood, otherwise they would have gone elsewhere) were doomed to be what, in their hearts, they longed to be. Second, third, or fifth-rate artists; who lacked the power, or the will, to create anything true or original or alive. In short – to reproduce.

'*Cowardly* buffoons, as well,' I said to Georgina, wagging my finger at her now, as we hurtled down the hill towards Mexico City. 'Who don't want to face up to the fact that they're living in the Duke of Mantua's court. Who don't even want to admit that they love the smell, the taste, the sight of blood. Or at any rate are fascinated by it. Or at any rate accept the fact that this is what they live on. So they go away to that hell-hole and make believe. San Miguel de Allende. Mexico's leading artists' colony. Ha. Ha!'

But I was wagging my finger at Georgina and lecturing her about cowards principally so that I could keep my eyes off the road. For so well was the car working now, and so pleased was its driver that we were nearly home, that she was driving faster than ever. And the traffic was very heavy on the highway into town, and the light had reached that point when it was neither night nor day, and after I'm not sure how many hundreds or thousands of kilometres, I was tired.

TEN

Indians . . .

After Georgina had dropped me off, and I had had a shower and a drink, and told José and Sonia about my trip, I went out to call Gerardo. ('Went out' because my hosts didn't have a telephone at home. Not, as seemed to be the reason why most people in this city didn't have a 'phone, because they couldn't get a line or a number from the 'phone company – they actually had both – but because, they said, they didn't like the telephone. At least this way, they said, we can have some peace when we're at home. A point of view I professed to understand but didn't appreciate when, as tonight, I had to go down to use one of the many telephones in the street; and spend my time hopping from foot to foot as, beneath me, rats hurried from one side of the sidewalk to another. From the iron grille that didn't entirely protect what was, by day, a tortilla shop, to the flowerbeds which lined the streets. Back and forth. Back and forth. As I tried to concentrate on what I was saying.)

'Good,' Gerardo said when he heard me. 'I was hoping you'd call tonight. What are you doing tomorrow?'

'Nothing. Writing up my notes.'

'Good. Well you can do that some other time. Now listen – what's the time now?'

I looked at my watch and jumped as a rat seemed about to investigate my shoes. 'Urrr,' I said. 'Ten-thirty.'

'Good,' Gerardo repeated a third time. 'Now listen. Go straight home. Go to bed . . . and set your alarm for six.'

'For *six*?'

'Yes.'

'Why?'

'Because tomorrow we're going to the country. And if we don't get an early start . . .'

If we didn't get an early start we wouldn't have time to get where we were going or do what we had to do once we were there.

And so, having come to a compromise about the time, at seven-thirty next morning – a limpid dazzling morning that made one feel this was still a country waiting to be discovered by Europe, so clear were the mountains at the end of every street, and so much did an old Indian woman in a brightly coloured shawl cross the deserted avenue with the air of one for whom traffic does not exist – I caught a bus to the centre. And there, at what was now eight-fifteen, I met Gerardo – and Miguel.

Miguel was the student Gerardo had told me about, who came from the village two hours away that, according to Gerardo, I might like to see. And it was to this village that we were now going to go.

About nineteen or twenty, he was a minute, dark-skinned young man who was so shy he never looked up when he spoke; and who spoke so quietly when he did that I found it impossible to understand a word he said. With the result that he ended up saying everything he wanted to say to me to Gerardo; who passed the message on.

'I think you're the first foreigner he's ever invited to his home,' Gerardo had told me on the 'phone last night. 'And he's very poor and afraid you won't like it.'

Nevertheless, when a collective taxi pulled up at the corner where we were standing, and around ten people rushed forward to claim the only three remaining seats in it, it was Miguel who, despite his stature and his shyness, stood in front of the door of the cab, and pushed those people away until Gerardo and I could clamber in under his raised arms. And it was Miguel who, as the taxi pulled away with those people left on the sidewalk still protesting, leaned back into his tiny portion of the seat, and murmured that that was the only way to behave in a situation like that.

'Besides,' he (apparently) added – not quite truthfully – 'we were the first.'

We took the *pesero* as far as Xochimilco; which, some fifteen miles to the south, is the city's flower market, and the only place anywhere near Mexico City where one can get an idea of what the old Aztec capital was like: being built on and among a system of canals. We had planned on hiring a boat and going round these floating gardens, since not only I, but Gerardo and Miguel too, had never seen them. However, by the time we got there it was so

full of tourists – and anyway was getting late – that we contented
ourselves with standing in a crowd in the main square watching
twenty or so Indians in feathers and capes and bells, performing
what was, a spokesman and commentator for them, claimed, an
Aztec dance; and I simply tried to translate or otherwise make
Miguel understand Thomas Beecham's dictum that the only two
things one should avoid in life are incest and folk-dancing.
'Incesto?' Miguel whispered, finally raising his eyes. 'Uh?' 'Si,' I
said, and pointed at the Aztecs. 'Y bailes tradicionales.' 'Uh,'
Miguel repeated, staring at me as if I were mad. 'Si,' I said again,
starting to sweat, and got Gerardo to help me. 'Ah si,' Miguel
nodded, and smiled politely. But still he gave me a very fishy
look, as if he weren't quite certain what he had so rashly invited to
his home.

Then we set off to find another collective taxi; that would take
us the rest of the way, up into the hills.

The last person into the taxi was a wrinkled, practically tooth-
less old man carrying a goatskin.

Miguel turned to me more shyly than ever. 'Mi abuelo' – my
grandfather – he said, before turning back to the old man, and
kissing his hand.

'Miguel!'

'And these,' Miguel murmured, indicating Gerardo and myself, 'are some friends of mine.'

'Olá,' the old man said. 'Olá, buenos dias.' And then, as the
taxi, now full, moved off, he started talking.

He hardly stopped all day.

I had imagined that it would be only a comparatively short ride
out of Xochimilco, since otherwise Gerardo, who was extremely
careful with his money, would have insisted on our taking a bus.
(Not that collective taxis were expensive – the standard cab fare in
Mexico City was only half the minimum London bus fare, and a
quarter of the New York bus and subway fare.) But instead, as
village followed village, and we caught the occasional glimpse of
Mexico City below us and behind us, we were in the cab – that
either had no springs, or had boards under the seats – for what
seemed like a day. I sat on my hands; I shifted from buttock to
buttock; I tried, even, hanging onto the rail which ran behind the
bench seat on which the driver and three other passengers sat, to
hold myself in a squatting position, and not sit at all.

And the whole time grandpa talked.

Finally however we arrived; the taxi pulling up on the main street of a village beneath a stretch of sloping ground, on which there were donkey sheds, a pig pen, various tarpaulins slung around wooden poles, ducks, geese and chickens – and the concrete shell of an unfinished two-storey house, that had a roof and windows, but no doors in the doorways, and an air of having been unfinished for several years.

'This is my home,' Miguel murmured, and gestured me up towards the shell.

'Please,' grandpa said, making the same gesture. 'Please come up, and come in.'

Up, and in, we went; into the cement-floored space of what must have been planned as a living room, but now was furnished only with two rickety wooden chairs and a table covered with goat-skins and agricultural tools, and was inhabited chiefly by the relatives of the ducks and geese to be seen outside. And from there we passed into what was clearly the principal room of the house; a kitchen dominated by a large table round which were sitting, chatting, various cousins and aunts and uncles of Miguel. (His parents, grandpa had told us on the way up, had gone away to a wedding, so we would not meet them). It was dominated still more, this kitchen, by a sternly handsome old woman who must have been, in her youth, and before she became merely handsome, very beautiful. She was Miguel's grandmother; whose hand he kissed as he had kissed his grandfather's. But if, in writing about the grandfather, I have found myself calling the friendly, talkative old man 'grandpa', I have no such inclination to call his wife 'grandma'. There was nothing of the grandma about this fine old woman, nor would there ever be. She was, she almost had written on her, a grandmother. And as we went into the room, and I felt tempted to follow Miguel's example – to bow my head before her, and kiss her hand (though, naturally, I didn't, and simply shook it) – I couldn't help but feel that not only was she now the centre and the mainstay of this family, but that she always had been, ever since her marriage. Moreover, that the very fact that we were there, and that we had met her husband in Xochimilco, depended not so much on Miguel's invitation or on the old man's desire to go down into town to sell some pulque, as on her desire for what had happened to happen, and on her consent for it to happen. (And Miguel later confirmed what I then began to suspect; that his parents – with his three brothers and a sister – had gone off for the day because, so far as he was aware, they hadn't even known he was coming. It was to his grandmother and his grandmother alone that he had applied – how I never discovered, since Miguel lived in a small room somewhere in the city and neither he nor his grandmother had a telephone – for permission to bring guests. And his grandmother, having told him yes, had either forgotten to tell anyone else, or, more likely, had not thought that it was anybody's business but her own.)

Having said hello to everyone in the family, we were sent out into the 'living-room' to sit on the two rickety chairs; and be talked to by grandpa until 'things' were ready.

'What kind of things?' I asked Gerardo, as a number of children appeared in the doorless doorway and on the concrete stairway that led up to the floor above, and stared at us.

'The baths, of course. I told you.'

'You mean we're going to have to *do* them, not just look at them?'

'Yes. I thought you realized.'

'No. No I didn't. But I haven't brought a towel or anything, and I haven't – but what's it like?'

'I don't know,' said Gerardo. 'I've never done them before either. But we'll see. In the meantime – shall we go and look at the village?'

'Yes,' I said, 'let's.' Because I had been having this brief conversation at the same time as I had been listening, and trying to understand, a long apparently endless story from the old man; and I thought that if we didn't leave the story might indeed be endless.

It took another ten minutes, however, with Miguel and practically his entire family standing about, shifting from one foot to another, sighing, coughing, clearing their throats and throwing out the occasional, tentative 'Abuelo . . . abuelo . . .' before we could get to our feet and to the door. And even then it is doubtful if we'd have escaped if grandmother hadn't become aware of our plight, and emerged from the kitchen long enough to do what no one else had liked or dared to do – silence the old man.

'That's enough,' she told him. 'They have come to see San Pablo, not to listen to your stories.'

Not a sound of protest did the old man make, and not a word
did he add to his story.

'Andale muchachos,' he waved us off. 'Andale.' And turned,
and shooed at a goose, and, without the least resentment,
followed his wife back into the house.

In fact, the village, ten thousand or more feet up, and loomed
over by the volcanoes, was – apart from the volcanoes, and the
blue sky and the cool air and a white-washed little church – fairly
unremarkable. Despite its sense, like a miniature version of
Oaxaca, of having a way of life that, notwithstanding the little
white church, had hardly been disturbed by invaders from
Europe or anywhere else, and had simply developed at its own
pace and in its own way. And it wasn't improved by my slipping
on a cobble-stone as we came out of the church, twisting my
ankle, and falling on my face, so that I was looking at the place
through eyes that if not obscured by pain, were at any rate
slightly blurred by discomfort.

Nevertheless, the trip – and the trip – served their purposes,
and by the time we had returned to the house, with me hobbling
between Gerardo and Miguel, 'things' were indeed ready, and
we were told that we were awaited at the baths.

My enthusiasm for this new experience was only slightly
lessened by my seeing that grandpa was to accompany us . . .

'The baths', that I had thought might be some sort of hot spring
running into a rudimentary pool, turned out, when we reached
them by walking down a small dusty lane and going into a small
dusty yard – a yard about the size of a pig-pen, and looking as if it
might once have been a pig-pen – to be a low mud and brick igloo.
By the side of which stood a wood-burning furnace whose smoke
emerged from a hole in the top, but whose heat was channelled,
through vents, into the igloo. And the process of bathing, I soon
gathered, consisted of the following. Of removing one's shoes
and socks and shirt. Of crawling through a very low entrance
– which was then half-sealed up – and handing out one's
trousers; which modesty, presumably, had dictated must be
kept on till one had got inside. (As modesty dictated that all the
time one was inside one kept on one's underpants or shorts or
whatever; though not, if one were a woman – and the igloo was
not segregated – a brassière, or any covering of the breasts). And
then of squatting, sitting, or if there weren't too many people

inside, lying on the straw with which the floor was covered, and putting up with the heat for as long as one could, as one scrubbed oneself with dried fibres from the cactus plants. The heat could be dry or wet, according to whether or not one sprinkled water on the vents through which it came, and thus created steam.

Or that would have been what bathing consisted of; and was, for the villagers who came in and sat for five, ten, fifteen or twenty minutes in the tiny, enclosed space. (While, outside, women heated great cauldrons of water over other wood fires, and passed in containers that varied in temperature from the nearly cold to the nearly boiling, which one poured over oneself, or rinsed oneself with, or simply splashed onto one's face). But for me, things were not quite as for the other villagers. Because grandpa knew a captive audience when he saw one, and decided that now he really had a chance to talk.

'Oh no,' Miguel whispered, as he saw the old man stripping down to a pair of drawers so large they reached below his knees, and start to make his way through the tiny entrance.

And 'Now you're in for it,' laughed Gerardo as he lay back and prepared to sleep.

And oh, was I.

Grandpa must have been in his eighties, and he had once been abroad. ('To Texas. To Arizona. To Colorado and Nevada and California. All the way up to Seattle. Working in the fields. In the nineteen twenties. It was there that I earned the money to buy my land. To build our house. I was sent there by the local priest. He used to get a commission on every worker he sent north.') I came from abroad – and either grandpa didn't hear me when I said 'Londres, Inglaterra,' or wasn't too sure where they were, simply assuming that everywhere abroad was the United States – and I was writing a book about Mexico. And somehow all this information got muddled up in the old man's brain, and emerged as the single fact that I wanted to know the details of every one of his eighty years, with particular emphasis on those he had spent away from home.

Which was all very well, and might, for a different listener who wanted to write a different sort of book, have been quite interesting. For certainly Miguel's grandfather, though garrulous, was as decent and straightforward and honest and good-humoured and

generous as one could have wished. But for me there were two
problems. One was that I had great difficulty following his
Spanish – not because, like Miguel, he spoke very softly, or was
shy, but rather because he rattled on at such a speed he would
have tended to confuse, not to mention lull into sleep, the most
fluent of Spanish speakers – and only understood perhaps fifty
per cent of what he was saying. And the other was that though
the old man was so thoroughly decent and, altogether, nice, his
life, very much like the village in which he had been born, raised,
and spent all his eighty odd years except those when he'd been
off working in northern fields, was unremarkable. Getting a little
education, having to leave his home for a while, coming back to
get married and start a family; and all the time working, working,
and working.

Yes, wonderful one thinks. Fascinating. But somehow . . .

For thirty minutes the old man kept it up, as I sweated and
dripped, felt more and more debilitated by the heat and the
stream of words, and wondered how, or if, I was ever going to get
away. Maybe, I thought, I will eventually have to send for his
wife. Or maybe she will guess what's going on, and come and
rescue me.

In fact it was desperation – and laughter – that eventually gave
me the strength to get onto my knees, smile, and say, even as he
was in the middle of a sentence, 'Excuse me, I must go out, I don't
feel too well' – and crawl out into the cold wind and hot sun of the
village, there to be clasped in towels by the women, have sheets
draped round me, and find myself being dumped on a straw mat
in one corner of the pig-pen. Desperation, laughter – and a fear of
going bald.

Though possibly strangely in the first two instances, if not so
strangely in the third, neither the desperation nor the laughter
were caused by the story-telling. Had I had to wait for that to
drive me out, I might have been in the igloo for an hour or more.
After all, I might have thought, he *may* tell me something I can
use. And besides, he means no harm.

No, what drove me out was something else, though also
something that was done by the old man. He meant it kindly, no
doubt, but he was getting on in years, and he was forgetful . . .

I had been sitting in the igloo for some five minutes, and was
back somewhere round the First World War – 'I was never

interested in that. Nor in the second. They were both wars between countries who were fighting for their own interests' – when suddenly Miguel's grandfather broke off his discourse and pointed at my head. 'La cabeza,' he muttered. 'La cabeza.' You must wash your hair . . . And so saying, he picked up a vase of hot water, poured it over my head, and, grabbing a large bar of what looked like home-made soap, began, vigorously, to lather and massage my scalp.

He was old, but his fingers were hard.

'Then, after the war –'

He scrubbed my hair for two or three minutes as he continued with his tale. Then he poured more water over it to rinse it, and indicated that I should stretch out.

'It's not so hot if you lie down,' Gerardo whispered, handing me a stone to rest my head on.

So I lay down, and so the old man droned on; and every now and then I nodded, and made an 'Is that a fact?' expression, or actually murmured 'Si?' or 'No?'

I wasn't exactly dozing, but on the other hand . . .

'La cabeza, la cabeza,' the old man said.

For a moment I thought he must be talking to Miguel or Gerardo, encouraging them to wash their hair too. Or to the silent, buddha-like man sitting sweating by the entrance, looking as if he were crying. But then I saw that grandpa was pointing at me.

Should I tell him he washed my hair just five minutes ago, I wondered, as Miguel muttered 'Abuelo,' stretched out a tentative hand, and then, seeing that his grandfather wasn't going to hear him, or wasn't going to listen to him if he heard him, returned his eyes to the straw, and smiled. But I felt too weak to protest or try to explain; and thought it would cost me less effort to have my hair washed a second time.

So I lifted myself up, out of the early 1930's, and once more submitted my scalp to those boney, work-hardened hands.

Ah well, I thought, we'll all be old and forgetful, one day.

By the time we had reached the late sixties my hair had been washed four times, and it was then that desperation made me risk rudeness, suddenly say 'Excuse me', and make my dash for the entrance. For the intervals between those cries of 'la cabeza, la cabeza' were becoming briefer and briefer, and I thought that if I stayed right up to the 1980's there would be no intervals at all. Just a continual scrubbing, until I hadn't a hair left.

Not that I needed to worry about giving offence; grandpa simply followed me out, and finished his story in the dust.

'And so here we are,' he concluded. 'Here we are. In 1984.'

Draped as I was with sheets and towels, I couldn't see the old man as he came to the end. But from the tone of his voice I fancied that he was gazing at my covered head; and that his fingers were twitching.

*

After an hour's rest, another – mercifully grandpa-less – twenty minutes in the igloo, and then another half hour rest, we went back to the house for lunch. A lunch for which Miguel's grandmother kept apologizing – 'I'm so sorry, this is only poor people's food. Forgive us, this is just the food of the people.' – but a lunch which consisted of about six large courses, was washed down with grandpa's home-made pulque and was served with blue tortillas, and of which the old woman wasn't in fact the least bit ashamed. Her continual sighs of 'Ah, this isn't what you get in town' were a mere formality; the dues she felt that country folk should pay to city folk. But city folk were meant to understand this, and not take her seriously. And if they did, that handsome old face seemed to say – woe betide them.

The day ended with our being sent upstairs to lie down; in any one of three bedrooms, and on any one of the double beds in each of those bedrooms. Great lumpy mattresses that had blankets or covers of some sort thrown across them; but mattresses that had no sheets, and in any case looked as if they had been – well, used for quite a while.

Still, I told myself as I flopped down on one, and almost immediately fell asleep, what's the point of being fastidious? And if I want to when I get home – I can always take a shower, and wash my hair . . .

*

I slept for an hour, being woken by a television that had been turned on on the other side of the room, and by the three small children who had turned it on.

Three children who I would describe in my notes next day as follows. 'Felipe: small, wizened, solemn, snotty-nosed, six years old but somehow already past his prime; the sort of child one feels has already had all the joy he's ever going to have in life and who, when one does manage to get a smile out of him by rolling one's eyes, and making faces, nevertheless smiles as if he is doing it to satisfy one and because he knows it is expected of him, rather than because he is amused. José: bright, mischievous, and though only five, already taller than Felipe; a boy who when we were introduced made a great show of not shaking hands – unlike Felipe, who did so instantly with an air of resignation – hiding behind his mother's skirts, and clinging to her legs, but a boy who within a minute was not only shaking both my hands, but wanting to hang onto them, and be lifted in the air. When I woke up in the bedroom after lunch, he stuck his fingers in my eyes, poked me in the nostrils, and, as I put on my glasses, breathed on the lens and asked me why I wore them.

'Because I can't see without them.'

'Will I see better with glasses?'

I perched them on the end of his nose and he laughed in delight, though presumably he couldn't see a thing.

And finally, another Miguel: who was eight years old, and, sitting in the bedroom watching José, Felipe and me, clearly considered eye-poking, breathing on glasses, and making faces things for five and six year olds. However, looking at his serious, handsome little face, one had the impression that even at six he had considered such games worthy of contempt. And so, probably, he would consider games all his life. He was not defeated, like Felipe; he would attempt to avoid the possibility of defeat by never playing.

And then, my duty in the way of child diversion done, my question as to what these three little boys must make of the American serial they were watching having been answered – 'Not very much,' I told myself, since the picture on the screen, albeit of a glossy, rich, enyachted and smartly dressed Los Angeles, was so grey and grainy as to be hardly visible, and must in any case have seemed a very murky dream compared to their own brightly lit and highly coloured world – I went downstairs and made my farewells; and prepared for the long and by now dark journey back into town.

'I'm sorry,' grandmother said yet again, 'that our meal was so poor.'

'No señora,' I told her. 'Of course it wasn't. It was wonderful. Wonderful.' Muy, *muy* rico . . .

'Come again,' grandpa said, 'come again whenever you like. And by the way, did I tell you –'

'Sssh,' hissed his wife, 'be quiet. They've got to go now.'

'Well do come again anyway,' the unchastened old man shouted out, as we made our way down through the hens. 'Any time you like.'

He waved.

'And if you can't – send us a postcard from London.'

ELEVEN

The South Americans

After the 1973 coup which overthrew the government of the Chilean Salvator Allende, the then president of Mexico Luis Eccheverria decreed that immigration and working regulations should be relaxed for any Chileans who were victims of political persecution, and wished to come to Mexico. His policy was continued by his successor, Lopez Portillo, and was extended to include Argentinians escaping from repression in their country.

This hospitality had three principal effects. First, and most obviously, it saved the lives of a great many people who might otherwise have lost them. Second, it suddenly made Mexico City into 'a sort of Athens' of Latin America, since most of those fleeing were academics, 'intellectuals', and artists. And third, it caused great resentment among many Mexican academics and intellectuals, who found that the positions they had been occupying, or the positions they had hoped to occupy, were now filled by South Americans; South Americans who, far from being grateful, were all merely patronizing, haughty and superb.

So, at any rate, I was told by almost every Mexican I spoke to.

'Chileans!' Mrs F had said, 'Communists! But they all have apartments in the best part of town. They all have two cars and a maid. And they all think they're better than us poor Mexicans.'

'Argentinians,' Enrique had told me in Philadelphia. 'Hmmm. They're the reason I had to come here.'

And 'Chileans, Argentinians,' Georgina had snapped at me one day in the car, as we were driving to Guadalajara. 'Really! They think we're all Indians!'

In which little remark one may hear half the history of Latin America . . .

Though it was also, as it happens, true.

*

A Chilean friend in London (who, otherwise the very model of a Latin-American liberal, had told me without batting an eyelid one day 'The Indians? Oh, they're all lazy and stupid') had given me the name of an old friend of his, who was now living in Mexico City. 'Call her,' he had said. 'You'll like her. She's fun.'

He had not, however, given me her 'phone number, since I had spoken to him only the day before I left, and he didn't have his 'phone book with him.

'It doesn't matter though,' he had told me. 'There won't be any problem. You'll find her easily enough.'

In a city of seventeen million people?

Naturally he was right.

The morning after my trip to San Pablo I was invited by Georgina to accompany her on a night out with the girls; 'the girls' in this case being two ex-colleagues of hers in television, colleagues who were, significantly, Colombian, and Chilean.

('You see. I'm the only Mexican and I get fired. Whereas they . . .'

'I thought you quit.'

'Well I did. But I was put into the position of having to quit. So in fact I was fired, wasn't I?')

The Colombian, deep-voiced, dark-haired, and with a fund of dirty jokes, was a solid, down to earth young woman, who one felt would put up with no nonsense, and about whom there was no nonsense. But the Chilean, who must have been about fifty, and was blonde, very elegant, very fragile and rather nervous – which was not surprising, since her husband had committed suicide the week before – was of a different school entirely. Although she claimed to love Mexico and to have no intention ever of returning to Chile, she was, everything about her discreetly murmured, altogether more European.

More conscious, that is, of her European background.

And she, 'but of *course*,' knew the woman I was looking for.

'All we Chileans know each other,' she said sadly, as if they constituted an aristocratic class she didn't altogether approve of. 'We're like a great big family.' She touched her fine-boned cheek with a pale be-ringed hand and smiled. 'I haven't actually seen her for more than a year. She was away. But we know each other. Oh yes. We all know each other.'

'Do you have her 'phone number?'

Thus it was that I met Eugenia, and through her the woman

who hadn't been out for ten years. And thus it was that I got to hear – hear more – about the ugliness of Mexicans.

Eugenia had been a professor of philosophy in Chile at the time of the coup; her husband, Fernando, a lawyer. She had found herself out of a job once the military had taken over; he, having attempted to defend those who were being arrested and thrown into jail, was arrested and thrown into jail. Eighteen months later he was released, deprived of his citizenship, and put on a plane to Italy.

They lived in Italy for four years; which Eugenia loved, but Fernando was less enthusiastic about. It was too far from Latin America.

In the winter of 1979 they left for Mexico.

'I hated it,' Eugenia told me. '*Hated* it.'

Provincial, boring, polluted, corrupt, and, naturally – full of ugly people.

After two years she could take it no more, and left; although Fernando had remained.

She had spent another year in Italy.

'And then,' she sighed, 'I came back.'

'And now?'

'Now I'm starting to like it. Or anyway, starting not to mind it. I've had a job – teaching the history of Mexican transport at one of the universities here! "But I'm a philosophy teacher," I told them. "I don't know anything about Mexican transport." "That doesn't matter," they said. "Nor does anybody else. Here, read this book. Then you'll be all right." "But in that case why can't the students themselves read the book?" I asked, and was given to understand that if I didn't keep quiet I wouldn't get the job. (But once I got it I didn't, and now I've lost it. I'm suing them for wrongful dismissal) – I've got to know a lot of nice people . . .'

('Mexicans?'

'Well some. But mostly South Americans.')

'. . . and I've started to get involved in politics again, and women's groups.'

'So you're settled. More or less.'

'Yes.' Another sigh. 'I suppose so. My only real regret is that before I left Fernando and went back to Italy we had a beautiful house in San Angel. Whereas now . . .' She looked around the modern, three-roomed apartment overlooking the State

University, where she and Fernando lived. 'Still, I shouldn't complain. Though I do wish the Mexican women were a little more – aware. It's so different after Italy – and Chile.' She paused, and looked at me, wondering whether she could say what she wanted to. Then she went ahead. 'And I do wish the people – the men in particular – were just a *little* more attractive.'

I didn't say anything.

'I mean some of the young ones are all right. And some of the old ones, in the country. You know, with their handsome old faces. But the rest of them – most of them . . .' Eugenia wrinkled her nose in dismay. 'Oh God,' she said. 'Really.'

And if I thought she shouldn't be saying things like that, she added, I should have a talk with her friend Lizaveta.

'But if she hates it here so much why does she stay?' I asked, after I had heard the story of the woman who didn't go out. 'I mean surely, anywhere . . .'

'Oh she's going soon. Back to Chile. She couldn't before, because her husband had a very good job here, and she was a communist.'

'And now?'

'She's fallen out with her husband, and she's become an ardent Pinochet supporter.'

'You're joking.'

'No I'm not. Better anything than staying here, she says. Better Hitler.'

'She's gone mad.'

'Well I suppose so – but really she's very nice. And she's very funny about it.' She nodded. 'You'll see.'

*

In a novel, a fifty-five year old woman who hadn't been out of her house for ten years, who had obliged her daughters to follow her husband round with a camera until they had managed to get a snap of him coming out of a hotel with his secretary (who had then been beaten up by the two girls; though that off their own bat presumably), and who lived in a smallish apartment with one of those daughters (who was in love with a sixty year old general who wore his medals when he came to dinner), and with at least three (though there may have been more) colossal cats, would be considered, by the reader, as somewhat gothic.

But in real life the only such woman I have ever met turned out to be, when I went round to her apartment, not gothic at all, and not only as easy-going and hospitable as Eugenia had said, but absolutely normal. Certainly she must have been mad, and she almost admitted as much herself. Yet, while neither denying her madness, nor in any way going along with her motives for keeping herself a prisoner, it was difficult not to like her.

She came to the door in a housecoat, and though she wasn't expecting us, didn't seem at all surprised to see us.

'Oh,' she said to Eugenia, 'it's you. Well just a moment. I've got a pie I'm putting into the oven, and if I leave it – come in, sit down, and I'll be with you in a minute.'

Plumpish, blondish, shrewd-eyed, she wandered back to the kitchen while we did as we'd been told, and her daughter came into the room and asked us if we wanted something to drink.

'Coffee tea whisky wine tequila coke or orange?'

But as she had said, within a minute Lizaveta had returned, and proceeded to do what she obviously – and rightly – felt was expected of her.

She asked where I was from. She nodded in a melancholy way when I told her, muttering 'Ah England, England' like an ageing French actress muttering 'l'amour, l'amour.' She told me how she envied me, how she had loved London on her one and only visit there, and how she hoped she would return one day. 'It is so *civilized*, England. And the English – they are so *civilized*.' And then, from this suitable board that she had set up for herself, she dived into what was not just her favourite subject but, one suspected, her only subject. (Though maybe, if she had known me better, she would have introduced the subject of her husband's infidelity as a counter-refrain. An infidelity which freed her of any obligation to him; and an infidelity which meant she could both go back to Chile if she wanted to, and could oblige him – if she so desired, as she probably did, and if she were capable of it, as she probably was – to accompany her.) And as she plunged – and her eyes lit up, and her expression became animated, and the jokes started coming, and everything about her spoke of the actress moving centre-stage into the lights – it became clear that in this sudden animation, this sudden transformation into a bright vivacious woman, lay the key to her obsession.

It became clear that, paradoxically, it was Lizaveta's madness that kept her sane.

Many years ago, I gathered, she had felt herself becoming as it were unreal. Perhaps her being forced into exile had done it. Perhaps the shaking of her Communist faith. Or perhaps something else that she wasn't aware of. In any case, if only for a day or two at the beginning, that feeling of hers had made her unwilling, or even unable, to leave the house.

('It's not agoraphobia?' I asked.

'Good God no,' she said, looking shocked by the idea. 'I love going out.')

After a while, as the feeling grew worse, she told her husband or a friend (it wasn't clear which) about it, saying 'You know I just didn't feel like going out today.'

'No?' her husband – or friend – had said, 'Why?'

And then, as she had started to give – or invent – reasons for her not wanting to go out – saying Oh the Mexicans are so this that or the other – and had seen the interest that her peculiarity aroused, she had felt, somewhere within her 'a little ember of reality start to glow.' An ember fanned, no doubt, by that interest. The following day she had stayed in again – she had again told someone – and the ember had glowed more brightly. A week later – as interest turned to irritation, and irritation to concern – the ember had started to burn. And soon – after a month, or after six months, and after Lizaveta had become known as the woman who wouldn't go out – the flame had filled her entirely. She was burning! She was blazing! She was real.

And so it had gone on, the length of time she had been a prisoner constantly stoking her fire, and the very fact that she could turn her story into myth keeping the flames high. Her husband went out to work, her daughters or a maid did the shopping, and she kept in touch with the world by watching the television or listening to the radio, and by spending hours looking out of her windows.

(Luckily she lived in a large apartment complex from which she could look out over hundreds of comings and goings, and look in through hundreds of other people's windows.

Eugenia: 'She knows *everything* that goes on in the place. You can't have a lover for five minutes before she's aware of it. You can't even be in bed with a cold.')

Obviously, as she herself must have realized, if the story had continued too long she would have gone permanently crazy; the madwoman she was playing to keep herself sane eventually ousting the sane woman who played her. And ten years, in her opinion, was getting near the limit. So she had got a hold over her husband with which, with any luck, she would be able to force him to leave Mexico. Then she had slowly divested herself of the beliefs that had, in all likelihood, been responsible for driving her into exile and unreality in the first place. And now, a free woman, a born-again fascist (she said with a smile, meaning 'You shouldn't take me too seriously'?) she was ready to be off. Back to the outside world. Back to Chile and sanity. Back, in short, to reality.

'Though I would prefer,' she murmured, glancing at Eugenia, 'Italy.'

'*Oh Italy, thou paradise of exiles* . . .'

'But I don't really care.' (This the short, hard hitting coda to her long aria.) 'Just as long as I get away from here. Because I've had enough of it here. I've had it up to here.' (A plump hand held high above her head.) 'Urrr,' she shuddered, and repeated, for the last time, her principal and constant theme. 'Ugly, ugly, *ugly*.'

*

The above can, perhaps, be seen as an illustration of my contention that Mexico is dangerous because it tends to make Europeans and those of European origin think of themselves as superior to 'the Indians'. (Though in Lizaveta's case, as Georgina had said was the case with South Americans, she thought of all Mexicans as Indians). Worse than that, it tends to reduce that feeling of superiority to a mere matter of aesthetics ('We are better because we conform to our own standards of beauty, and are white; they are inferior becaue they do not, as a rule, conform to our standards of beauty, and are brown'). But my other contention, that Mexico encourages the pretence in Europeans that they do *not* in any degree feel themselves culturally – if not aesthetically – superior, and thus exposes them to a still greater danger, – that of intellectual dishonesty – may be illustrated by an incident that took place that evening, after we had left Lizaveta's.

We had gone round to another friend of Eugenia's – a Chilean union leader who lived nearby and was, as Eugenia gaily and apologetically informed me, 'working-class' – to have a drink. I was then to be dropped off at the nearest Metro station, while the union leader, Eugenia, and three or four other people were to go on to some meeting.

Mario, Eugenia's friend, was a dark-haired, pale-skinned, thick-set and obviously serious man in his mid-thirties. He welcomed us into his apartment – almost identical to Eugenia's – finished a discussion he was having with his fair-haired, pale-skinned and obviously serious son of nine (who called him Mario) about what homework the boy should be doing, and offered me a drink. Then he flopped down into a chair, swept back his hair with his hand, and, giving an almost inaudible burp, told me, à propos of what I wasn't sure, 'I'm working class.'

I also wasn't sure whether I was meant to congratulate him, or commiserate with him.

Still, despite this odd introduction, he was a pleasant enough man; from whom I learned, in the following ten minutes, something about the problems that unions, and union members, have in present-day Chile. But it wasn't till the arrival of two of those other people who were going with him and Eugenia to the meeting, that the conversation returned to Mexico. One of the new-comers was a woman – a straight-haired, rather earnest young woman, who looked as if she might have been a nun in another life – and the other was a man in, I would guess, his mid-sixties. He wore a very well-cut light-grey silk suit, a discreet tie and expensive shoes; and his white hair was swept carefully back off his forehead. He was a professor, Mario told me as he introduced us (meaning: he's *middle*-class), and I wasn't altogether clear whether he was Chilean or Mexican. In any case he accepted a drink, sat down next to me, and went through the usual motions of asking where I was from, telling me that England was so civilized, and enquiring what I had done since I had arrived. His almost over-eager listening and slightly absent eyes were, however, a little disconcerting, since as I gave him my replies I found it hard not to wonder exactly what he was thinking – consciously or otherwise – in that apartment, and in this company. Did he feel he was, however minimally, slumming it? Did he feel that 'in the ideal world for which we are all striving there are no such things as class-distinctions or, it goes without saying, distinctions of any other kind'; but that it would have been hypocritical of him to try to disguise his own background and upbringing by *not* wearing a well-cut grey silk suit, by not behaving with the faintly patrician charm in which his upbringing had trained him? Or did he feel nothing at all, except that he was here, with friends, and they were off to a meeting for the good of Chile? It was impossible to say, but it was difficult not to be curious.

Still, the conversation went well enough, and in any case was not likely to go on for very long, as Mario was already starting to look at his watch, and making moves towards departure. But then I started telling the professor about the day before yesterday, and my visit to San Pablo. And with that, communication broke down entirely.

Initially, as I said 'an Indian friend of a friend', 'an Indian village', 'Indian baths', I thought it was my choice of word the man disapproved of, or didn't understand. I had said 'Indiano', and 'Indianos', in Spanish, which, Georgina had already told me, meant, strictly speaking, an Indian or Indians from India. But I thought this preferable to 'Indio', or 'Indios', which I had heard from other people was now considered derogatory; even though this was generally used by the Mexicans themselves when talking about – as they say in the States at the moment; next year who knows? – 'native Americans'.

Should I have used this latter term I wondered as the professor leaned forward with a studiedly puzzled expression on his elderly actor face, and said 'What?'

But 'native Americans' sounds clumsy, and is – though this is, perhaps, neither here nor there – inaccurate. Every 'American' born in 'America' is native American. Added to which I wasn't sure, had I wanted to use the adjective, whether I should follow it with 'American' or 'Mexican'. Absolutely correct I couldn't be, since I didn't know what particular family, tribe, race or nation of Indians Miguel and his family belonged to or descended from; although I imagined it was a mixture of a number, and that they themselves didn't know. Certainly they spoke only Spanish, and didn't seem to have any particular cultural allegiances other than to 'Mexico'.

As was, no doubt, the point that the professor was trying to make. And yet, as I stammered, blushed, and fumbled around trying to find some way of getting across the information that two days ago I had taken a bath in the sort of bath-house that had been used by certain peoples in this part of the world for the last thousand or two thousand years, I felt for a second a sense of panic.

'Baños *indianos*?' the professor said, with a look of pity on his face, as if he had suddenly realized I were disabled.

'Un pueblo *indiano*?' shaking his head as if to say 'My dear fellow, I'm terribly sorry –'

'Un amigo *indiano*?'

Eventually I gave up, seeing that this game could be kept up indefinitely.

'No,' I said, telling him what he wanted to hear. 'A *Mexican* friend, a village in the hills beyond Xochimilco – ummm – communal baths.'

'Ah,' said the professor, nodding at me with an 'There you see it wasn't difficult was it?' expression, 'how interesting.'

My momentary sense of panic was caused partly by the man's absurd pretence at non-comprehension, and the way he set about getting me to say what he wanted me to say. ('Please,' I wanted to tell him – or wished afterwards I had told him – 'if you think my language derogatory or insulting, say so, and I'll either agree with you or disagree with you. But don't, whatever you do, *simper*.') But more, it was caused by my realization that this man had solved the problem of his feelings about 'the Indians' not merely by refusing to use or understand certain words that described them, but by pretending to himself – and obliging, or attempting to oblige other people to pretend – that the Indians of Mexico did not exist. There *were*, for him, no Indians. There were no such people as Mayans, Totonacs, Zapotecans, Aztecs; nor even such people as their descendants, or people who were part Maya, Totonac or Zapotec. There were only *Mexicans*, only, I'm sure he would have liked to put it, people – all just the same, my dear fellow, as you or I.

The Indians did not exist . . .

An admirable sentiment, possibly, in theory, and, from a certain point of view, a desirable sentiment. Only – it was not, for the present, anyway, true. There *were* Indians in Mexico, and they were, for the most part, the poorest, the worst-fed, and the least healthy and well-educated members of the community.

And why were they so?

Because they stuck to their old ways and would not or could not adapt to the new ways?

Yes.

Because they still lived, as a rule, in the country where it was more difficult for the benefits of work, and an adequate income and diet, and medical attention and schools, to reach them?

Yes, that too.

But principally because for four hundred years, men and women had been telling themselves, for a variety of reasons, that the Indians did not exist.

Some because they considered such people without souls.

Some because they considered that being outside the principal – outside *their* – cultural stream, (being, that is, in their opinion, culturally irrelevant), such people did not indeed exist.

And some, like the professor, because if the Indians did not exist – why, there was nothing to worry about. 'We are all merely people, and when the ideal state comes about in which we are all merely people, and there are no distinctions of any sort, everyone will be fed and clothed and healthy and well-educated. (Educated, naturally, according to our theories. To our advanced superior theories of European descent. And if there is any Indian who wishes to hang onto the remains of his or her culture, he or she will have to be taught: No my child, you are not an Indian.) That way I do not have to worry about my smugness. I do not have to worry about my grand patrician charm. I do not have to worry about all the arrogance, blindness, the history that has made me what I am. For if the Indians do not exist – I do not exist, either. Not me as a smartly dressed Chilean or Mexican professor. No, I am just a person, as they are; a *person*, without cultural background, without a position in society, without a past.

That way, you see, I am free . . .'

Lizaveta had been kept indoors for ten years by her beliefs, and was now, she claimed – though I wondered whether she would actually do it – going back to General Pinochet's Chile.

But the professor had fiddled with the truth.

TWELVE

A Wednesday Of Flower . . .

After that not very enjoyable evening, and having been told by Georgina that she couldn't leave for another trip until next Tuesday at the earliest, I spent the following six days 'continuing my research into the Mexican spirit'. (As I told Georgina when she asked what my plans were.) Research which involved going to see a zarzuela show, going to visit a famous painter's house, and going to an exhibition of works by David Hockney; determined, in my mind, to compare – favourably – the English artist with his Mexican colleagues. (Ah, I thought, now we'll see some wit, some irony. Some of those spirited hardy plants that grow in the ground between the what-is and the what-could-be, and are a product of that gap. Hardy plants that contrast so sharply with the flowers of the Mexican only what-is.)

I also concluded, so to speak, my journey in the past, had one totally wasted day, and had another that might have been better if it had been.

But before I did any of these things I witnessed what I believed to be the end of a little poetic tragedy; a little poetic tragedy that had started a few days earlier and would have its epilogue only at the end of my six days of research. It was a little poetic tragedy that took place not fifty yards from my front door; and it turned out to be, in retrospect, the most cheering event of the week.

*

On Sunday morning, before going off to San Pablo and the baths, I had seen an old Indian woman crossing Baja California, the six-lane highway a block behind where I was staying. As I have said, her air of there being no such thing as traffic, and the sharply defined mountains at the end of every street, made me feel that the city had become, in a sense, invisible.

On Monday morning, when I went out to buy the paper, I saw the old woman again; though this time in Tepic, my own street. She was half way between José and Sonia's house, and In-

surgentes; and she was sitting on the grass verge opposite a
school, sorting, and surrounded by, flowers. Carnations, irises,
chrysanthemums; freesias, roses and lilies. What made me slow
down and look at her was not just my having seen her the
morning before, but also my being unable to work out what she
was doing with the flowers. They were all, like her, well past their
prime; and she didn't, as I passed by, offer to sell me any. But if
she wasn't sorting them into bunches for some other flower-
seller, who maybe had a stall nearby, and if she wasn't selling
them herself – what was the point of her operation? Sorting for
the sake of sorting?

Oh well, I thought as I kept on down the street, there's
probably some very simple explanation, even if I won't ever
know what it is. And anyway – it's not that important. She's just
an old woman sorting flowers.

On Monday night, after my evening out with the girls,
Georgina's Chilean friend had given me a lift home, so I didn't
see if the old woman was sleeping on the verge.

But on Tuesday morning when I went to buy the paper she was
certainly still there – or there again – and still sorting her flowers;
which by now had drooping heads and shrivelling petals, and
looked to be the same as yesterday's. If they were, she must have
been re-sorting them, since while there were maybe a couple of
hundred, the task couldn't have taken her that long.

I made a mental note to look out for her when I went to have
lunch, and in fact saw that at three o'clock she was in the same
position, though no longer sorting. Simply sitting there, surrounded by her neatly stacked flowers. The carnations dark red.
The irises still just purple. The chrysanthemums still just white,
but with brown centres by now, and brown leaves.

They were dying.

That evening, having been dropped off at the Metro by Eugenia
and friends, I walked home from the other direction; past the
running track, past the tennis courts and the social club where
people could be heard dancing to the Blue Danube, and down the
street where the rubber trees looked like muggers and two dogs
always snarled at me. So again I didn't see whether my old
flower-sorter was sleeping on the verge.

But the morning after that I saw that she was dead. She was
lying on the grass; a tiny motionless bundle, covered with a bright

shawl. And around her, spread out in a perfect circle, lay her flowers.

They too were dead.

So that was what she had been doing, I thought. Making herself a wreath.

I paused, wondering who would come and clear up this little collection of debris, that looked, now that life had gone from it, as if it could all be contained in a not very large plastic bag. And then, as the students opposite whooped and shouted as they played basket ball in the school-yard, or sat on their cars tapping their feet to Michael Jackson and Boy George, I continued on my way.

THIRTEEN

. . . *And Song*

For several days I had seen posters advertising 'The Best of Zarzuela' all over town. 'With José Antonio and his company.' Never having been to any live performance of this Spanish operetta, I reasoned that if I had heard both opera and mariachis I should now, as it were, sample the middle-ground. So I decided, after a day spent thinking about the old woman (whose remains had disappeared by the time I went out to eat) to take myself off to the Teatro de la Ciudad, to hear how good – or bad – José Antonio was.

That the ticket cost three times what the best opera ticket cost (admittedly that was only three dollars) should have warned me not to expect too much. It should also have made me think that this was a company that intended to cash in as much as they could as quickly as they could, and then leave town, knowing that no one would be coming back for a second look. And when I read the posters properly, and saw that the evening was announced as an 'Anthology of Zarzuela and Spanish Dancing', I should have been more doubtful yet; and prepared not just for the bad, but for the worst.

Still, the theatre, when I got inside, was handsome enough in an elegant, neo-classic way; and the audience, though here too almost exclusively white, didn't in any way make me feel uncomfortable. On the whole it was composed of families, hoping in their generally quiet, diffident and by now I had come to think very Mexican way, to enjoy themselves. Though not, perhaps, expecting to.

Right, their faces and the set of their shoulders seemed to say, we've done our bit by coming here and filling this place. Now if you'll just do yours . . .

And this remained the mood throughout the thankfully not very long evening.

Now if you just do yours . . .

Now if you'd just do yours . . .

Now if you'd just done yours . . .

Oh well – we didn't really expect to enjoy ourselves that much, and all in all – it wasn't really bad. One or two bits were actually quite pleasant.) Though even at its best – it never got going, did it?

But never mind, and while we won't come back to see you again, it was one way of passing an evening. And even if we didn't enjoy it very much, we don't really regret having come. I mean the tunes themselves were pretty enough – and those four girls . . .

Those four girls – four of the dancers in the 'Bailes españoles' that came between the songs – were the only bright spots in the whole evening. Young, attractive, with good backs and well-held arms, they were the only members of the cast who looked as if they had any hope of ever leaving the company; of ever doing something better. Indeed from the proud smiles they gave as they received their applause (as if to say: thank you, and that for recognizing that we don't really belong here) they gave the impression that they would be off any day now. But as to the rest – there hung, over all their endeavours, the pall of the pathetic if not the sad, the whiff of the 'We're old and weary' if not of the grotesque. That went for José Antonio himself, who in his day must have been a good, even a very good dancer, but now was too thick, too old, and too obviously straining himself, for 'Maria', his partner, who also must once have been a good dancer but now looked as if she wished she were at home with her feet up, for the fat tenor with the thin voice, for the soubrette of sixty, for the loud crude baritone who thought it was up to him to hold the show together, and for the mezzo-soprano who thought she could make up in character what she now lacked in voice. They would have made a wonderful subject for a film, one told oneself as one watched, and listened, and either winced or smiled in embarrassment or encouragement. The troupe of dancers and singers for whom, probably, their appearance in Mexico City was the highlight of their year. Trailing, for the rest of the time, round small towns in Ecuador and Peru, and maybe, if they were Spanish, putting on a show for the tourists in the summer, in Torremelinos, or Alicante. Keeping smiling, keeping going; ageing, plucky and exhausted. Oh, the back had long since given out, the feet were generally swollen, and menopause was just a memory now. But still, on a good night – I can still click a mean pair of castanets, I can still hit a high D. Okay, it's a bit shrill now, but what are you doing? Sitting in your living room in front of the television, waiting to die. Or pottering about your garden or your balcony. At least I'm still on the road. At least I can still put on a show. At least I'm still – alive.

So Olé, Olé, and – Oh God I'm so tired, and so broke, and so sick.

Click. Click. Click.

Yet – despite this aura of old troupers never giving in, of old show-business clichés being paraded before one's eyes, it was difficult not to share the general opinion that one didn't really regret having come.

Because the girls *were* attractive and good dancers and made one feel they were destined for something better. Because the tunes, in their sweet and empty way, *were* pretty; in the fashion of paper streamers, left over from a party. And because, thanks to that very element of cliché, one *could* make up a story as one watched, and tell oneself a tale of people carrying on regardless. A little band of players, whose never-ending journey and tacky show almost had to be seen as a metaphor for 'the human condition'.

On the road . . .

When I got home that evening I played dominoes with José and Sonia for a couple of hours, and won three hundred pesos. Then I went to my room and wrote some notes on the show. 'Like Johann Strauss being played in Piazza San Marco in Venice, like Gilbert and Sullivan being sung in a damp English seaside town, there was something so old and over and used about it one felt it was the end of the world.'

And then I went to bed; and slept.

FOURTEEN

A Journey In The Past (Concluded)

My account of the second half of the journey I had made through Mexico four years before was prompted by Gerardo's asking me, as we made our way across Chapultepec Park to see the Hockney show, where I was going to go with Georgina next week, and – when I told him – why I wasn't going to return to the south.

'Partly,' I said, 'because I liked it so much last time that I feel it would be a mistake to go back – in case I liked it less this time. And partly because I want to go everywhere this time that I didn't go before – and so get an idea of the whole country.'

At which Gerardo asked me why I *had* liked the south so much.

'Why does *every*one who comes here?' he said.

'I'm not sure,' I told him then, as I thought back over those weeks after Patty had left us. When I had travelled with Enrique through the states of Yucatan and Quintana Roo, through Tabasco to Ciudad del Carmen and Lake Catemaco – once the centre of the Olmec world, and thus the first centre of civilization anywhere in the Americas – and ended up in a faded grand hotel in Fortín de las Flores; a faded, misty hill-town famous for the cultivation of gardenias.

'But I suppose – for me – there were several reasons.'

There was the sky, for a start. A sky which was vaster than any sky I have ever seen. A colossal blue empty – space, dotted with little flat-bottomed white clouds, that looked as if they were resting on top of it. A space so huge that it gave one the impression of having crushed the land beneath it, and made one feel that that green flat land stretched away not just as far as the eye could see in every direction, but much, much further. Stretched away to the very edge of the earth . . .

(Across this apparently endless expanse of scrubby woodland, or stunted jungle, the grey road ran perfectly straight, with yellow flowers growing on either side of it; and above it, very very high, like tiny black dots beneath the clouds, vultures circled, constantly on the look out for food.

Occasionally, as one drove along, one saw one of these birds on the grey straight road in front, finishing off a decomposing skunk, or some other animal. But though they hardly seemed able to flap up off the tarmac before the car was on them, they also seemed to know that, when it came to it, it was you who had to go slower, not they who had to hurry. If you didn't, and you hit one, it might well smash straight through your windscreen. And if that happened, not only would your face and your car be filled with shattered glass, shattered bird, and the putrid remains of whatever the bird had been feeding on at the time, but you might equally well veer off the road, and crash. And there, under that great sky, provide a meal for the other, waiting vultures.)

Then there were the ruins, and the remains, and the pyramids. The great sites like Chichen Itza and Uxmal, which, in their magnificence and ability to awe, were comparable only to the Parthenon in Athens, and owed much of their magnificence and awesomeness to their being seen beneath that magnificent, awesome sky; to their seeming to cry out to the emptiness: 'This is our stand against your space'. And the smaller sites like Kabah, Sayil and Labna; which remained in the mind less for their monuments than for the egrets standing in the long grass at the base of their crumbling pyramids, and for the iguanas sunning themselves on their stones. As well as, incidentally, for the fact that when we drove up to the most deserted and out of the way of them, and parked the car, the watchman came out of the frond-roofed hut in which he lived with his wife and children, and seeing Enrique, said in a quiet, composed way 'Hello, how are you, how have you been?' exactly as if he knew him.

As, Enrique explained to me a minute later, after greetings had been exchanged, in fact he did.

'You see – I've been here before. Three years ago . . .'

Then there were Isla Mujeres and Tulum; the former a tiny island in the Caribbean where one could swim in still, green coral pools while just five yards away a stormy sea was crashing down on the other side of the reef; the latter, with its flat-topped pyramid built on the cliffs above the Caribbean, the last of the three great – or the three most famous – Maya sites. When we got there late one afternoon, a flight of pelicans moved slowly across the sky; their white feathers stained pink by the setting sun . . .

But finally, and above all, there was Cobá; an area more than a town just thirty miles inland from Tulum. And if any one place had to be named, any one reason given for my loving the south of Mexico, then Cobá would have to be it.

It does not figure very large on any tourist map of the area, and indeed if visited at all is visited principally by tourists from Can-Cun, who are bored with lying on the beach and don't mind the eight to ten hour round trip. Or, by people who, having come as far as Tulum, think they might as well take a trip into the interior to see what that has to offer. Or by, of course, the French; who go everywhere. And even for most people who do go there it must prove a little disappointing; there not being a great deal 'to be seen'. (Though not disappointing for everyone. Determined as I was not to read or re-read any books about Mexico before writing my own, I nevertheless broke my vow one day long enough to flick through a paperback I saw in a bookshop. And what one place should the author nominate as his favourite spot in Mexico? Yes – Cobá.

What was more curious, and added to my sense that there was some sort of pattern in my Mexican enterprise was that I discovered, soon after, that the book had been written, under a pseudonym, by the father of a friend.)

But for me . .

It started with the advantage of making me feel it had saved my life.

We arrived in Tulum around five; observed our flight of pelicans and stood on the cliff-edge looking down at the silver-surfaced debris-strewn sea; and wandered round the site without any particular hurry. We would, we had decided, stay the night in a hotel there, and drive back to Vallodolid the following day.

'Cobá?' I said to Enrique, looking at my map.

'No,' he said, shaking his head. 'I don't think there's much to see there.'

The trouble began when we couldn't find a hotel in Tulum. There were some straw-roofed cabins for rent, with bare – and dirty – mattresses, and gaps between both the roof and the walls, and the earth and the walls. There was what called itself a motel, which had cracked windows and peeling paint, and clearly hadn't been open for years. And there was a trailer and camp site situated between the beach and the road going into the village of Tulum (which consisted only of a few souvenir shops, a couple of bars and restaurants, and of huts selling soft drinks and Kodak film). A site that appeared to be home to some ageing American hippies who looked as if they were still trying to get together the money to leave both Tulum and the sixties, and to the ubiquitous French. But of a hotel where one had a chance of getting a night's sleep without being bitten or otherwise molested by wildlife, or of some place that didn't look as if it would endanger one's health, there wasn't, so far as we could see, a trace.

('What do you mean?' another friend who went there the year after told me. 'We stayed in a wonderful place right on the beach. And I'm more squeamish than you.')

What were we to do? It had taken us four hours to drive down from Can-Cun, and to our knowledge we hadn't passed a hotel in the last three of those hours. The road, like every other road in Yucatan and Quintana Roo, had been practically deserted in the day, and would be utterly so at night. Besides, one was told everywhere, one shouldn't drive after dark. Not anywhere in Mexico, some people said, but particularly not here, where there were neither gas stations, nor villages, nor people.

Just the great black sky.

And the only other alternative seemed to be to press on south, and hope we found somewhere before we got to Chetumel, or Belize.

But that was unlikely, and from the map, Chetumel and Belize were a long way away. Even further, in the other direction, than was Can-Cun.

'Perhaps,' I said to Enrique, 'we can sleep in the car.'

'Yes,' he said. 'If necessary we'll have to. But even that, round here, isn't a particularly good idea.'

He didn't specify why; but I had no difficulty imagining.

We ended by deciding to head back towards Can-Cun; trusting that we had overlooked a place on the way down.

'There must have been *something*.'

But then, as we waited at the junction of the road to Tulum, and the coastal highway, I saw it. A large weatherbeaten billboard, with a sign painted on it that was so faded as to be almost indecipherable. Almost, but not quite.

'Modern hotel,' it read. 'All conveniences. Just forty-five minutes from here. At Cobá.' Underneath was a large arrow.

'There!' I said to Enrique. 'You see!'

'Yes,' Enrique said. 'I do. I see that it's faded and falling down, that the hotel's probably been closed if it was ever open, and – do *you* see where the arrow's pointing?'

'Yes,' I said, and looked again.

Inland. Straight into the jungle . . .

'And when they say forty-five minutes – that's probably if you're flying. It probably means an hour and a half at least. And who knows what the road is like.' He leaned down and peered out of the window, at the large red sun hanging just above the darkness that bordered the road.

'Also in another fifteen, twenty minutes, it's going to be night.'

'Yes,' I said, 'I know,' trying to sound more confident than I felt. 'But it probably *is* only forty-five minutes away, and in this climate any billboard would be faded after a month. And if there's one hotel there are probably two, and if not – anyway,' I said, 'I don't see that we have any real alternative. So come on – let's risk it.'

'Live dangerously,' I added more doubtfully, as Enrique raised his eyebrows, gave a small shrug, and moved the car slowly forward. 'Live dangerously.' But I took a cigarette from my pocket, and lit it . . .

The first twenty minutes of the drive were uneventful, if a little disturbing. For on either side of the straight and narrow road the jungle grew in what looked, in the now failing light, to be one solid block of vegetation; a long solid block that became, as the light failed, ever more the jungle of one's nightmares, an area of darkness that contained – everything. Also, if the other roads in the south we had drived along had been deserted, this one looked as if no car had ever passed along it. All the same, we were making good progress, and with any luck in another twenty, twenty-five minutes . . .

I lit another cigarette.

And then, suddenly, at the end of those first twenty minutes, within seconds of each other, two things happened. And all at once, far from simply driving through a nightmare, we were caught right in the middle of one.

The first thing that happened was that just as Enrique had predicted, the sinking sun sank, and from one moment to the next we were in the night; in a black, tropical lightless night, with the screams and the squawks and the cries of the night all around us. And the second thing that happened was that even as our eyes were adjusting to the instant blackness, the car gave a heave, a terrible clanking sound was added to the shrieks of nature, and while we didn't quite stop, we found ourselves grating along at between three and five miles an hour, with every moment the engine threatening to die completely. Slower, I thought, than any animal who might come bounding out of the darkness, after us.

And so began what I was to think of as the second – the plane ride to Palenque being the first – of my Mexican trials.

'Close your windows,' Enrique hissed at me as he leaned over the wheel, willing the car not to stop completely. 'We don't want things flying in.'

Nor people either, I thought, as I did as I was told.

Because already, before the light had gone, Enrique had told me – truthfully, untruthfully? I didn't know, but I believed him anyway – that there were bandits and the occasional guerilla in this zone; up from Belize, across from Guatemala. And I knew for myself, from the reading I had done, that the Indians of this part of the world had never been particularly well-disposed towards whites; their hatred of the invading Spanish having broken out in the War of the Castes in 1847, and having survived, despite defeat, the slaughter of up to two thirds of their number, and their incorporation into the Mexican state, until the 1920's; when there were still instances of attacks on the Creole and Mestizo community. All right, we were – just – into the 'eighties now, and some fifty years had passed. But here, I suspected, fifty years did not count for much.

Then 'You do realize we can't stop on this road, don't you?' Enrique muttered, not quite accusing me of being responsible for the mess we were in, but not allowing me to forget that it was thanks to my insistence that we were here.

'I mean – if we do – we can't leave the lights on for more than ten minutes or the batteries will give out. But if we don't – anything that does come along here will be going fast – and unless the driver's got good eyesight or quick reflexes – he's liable to smash right into us.'

'And we obviously can't get out and walk – that *really* wouldn't be safe. (Besides, where would we walk to?) And without light there's no way we can fix the car ourselves.'

Another cigarette.

'And anyway, whatever's wrong, it's obviously something serious, so I doubt that we could fix it ourselves.'

It was very hot in the closed car, and sweat was running into my eyes . . .

'What do you suggest?' I murmured – huskily.

'I don't know. I just don't know. I suppose we could turn round and try to get back to Tulum – though it'll take two or three hours going at this speed. But I'm afraid that if we do try to turn round – I'd have to stop the car. And if I do stop – on the other hand, if we keep going – what are we going to find in the end? I mean – there's no guarantee that we're going to find anything.'

Bright little eyes watched us from the road or from the roadside, dazzled by the headlights. But only occasionally did we see the body – trundling across the exposed tarmac, or standing, transfixed, before us – to which those eyes belonged. ('Don't slow down,' I shouted, as Enrique automatically braked in order to avoid some largish animal we were in danger of hitting. 'Kill it. Kill 'em all. It doesn't matter. Just as long as we don't stop!') Normally, it was just the eyes . . .

On we went, and on – having concluded that it was better to risk finding nothing at the end of this road, than to start doing the manoeuvres necessary to get us facing in the opposite direction.

On, and on, and on. And all the time it was getting hotter in the car, and all the time I smoked; and all the time my stomach felt weaker; and all the time we were watched.

After two hours we suddenly came to a fork in the road. We had no time to consider which choice to make, and there were, it goes without saying, no signs.

'There, that one!' I shouted, seeing that one of the arms of the Y seemed in slightly better condition than the other; and off we heaved on what was now not only quite possibly a road to nowhere, but the wrong road to nowhere.

And the longer we drove the more the car shook and bucked, as if we were continually running over largish animals; and the longer we drove the deeper we got into the jungle.

And then, as suddenly as darkness had fallen and the engine, it sounded, had fallen out, the road ended. There was a circular clearing in the trees; there were huts with one or two torches burning amongst them, and at least some signs of human life; and there was nothing else. That is – as the car advanced across the clearing, and at any moment would have to be stopped, I didn't, to begin with, see anything else. But just at the last moment I made out a track between the trees, and a small wooden sign on which was printed 'Hotel'. 'Look,' I pointed. 'Down there.'

'We can't,' Enrique protested; but he swung the wheel round anyway. Thus, to the danger of the engine falling out, we added the danger of the engine being ripped out. Because still we couldn't slow down, and what before had been a tarmac road was now a rutted, stone-strewn obstacle course. But at this stage I didn't care any longer, and nor, I think, did Enrique. Oh let the damn thing fall to bits, I thought, as the sound of stone against metal was heard, and to the heaving and the bucking was added crashing and scraping and banging. 'I mean really – what does it matter?'

We turned a corner, branches brushed against the windows and the roof, we turned another corner – and then, as if we had woken from our nightmare – or passed from bad dream to good – suddenly, everywhere – lights. Lights in the trees. Lights illuminating a garden. Lights shining out over a black lake. The hum of a generator. And there, built on the edge of the lake, and bright, and modern, and shining – a hotel.

We were on a gravel drive! We had made it!

We stopped.

My knees almost gave way beneath me as I made my way down the drive to the marble steps and glass doors of the hotel. And I could feel my T-shirt clinging to me, and my jeans wet on the back of my legs.

All we need now, I thought, is to be told there isn't any room. Or that the hotel, obviously new, isn't open to the public yet.

But I need not have worried. Because almost immediately I had passed into the marble lobby and was standing in front of a boutique selling Indian-style costumes – a boutique, here, after all we've been through! – I heard footsteps on the stairs leading down into the lobby. And looking up, I saw what was so much like a vision that I almost laughed.

A tall thin vision, with short blonde hair and a glowing tan. A vision who was wearing a white silk blouse, black trousers, and very high-heeled gold slippers A vision who smiled when she saw me, and instantly made me confident that this place was both open and had rooms. And a vision who, as she came towards me, thrust out a hand and said 'Bon soir monsieur.'

The French, thank God, go everywhere.

Next morning, naturally, my fears of the night before seemed so ludicrous as hardly to bear thinking about. Here we were in a splendid hotel that really would have been, in a car that was working, just forty-five minutes from the coast; a coast that was one of the principal tourist areas of Mexico. We were not only, along with six or seven other tourists staying there, extremely comfortable and eating food that was prepared by a French chef, but Madame's husband padded out to our abandoned vehicle in his Gucci moccasins, opened the bonnet, and pushed his gold chains back inside his shirt long enough for him to look at the engine, identify the trouble, and assure us that he would be able to mend it for us just as soon as he had changed his clothes. And while we were surrounded on every side by jungle, it was not at all, in the light of day, fearsome jungle, nightmare jungle, but rather woody, pleasant, airy jungle, jungle that contained, what was more, not only a number of Maya stelae and carvings, but even a pyramid or two.

And I, I thought, was frightened of coming *here*?

We went to – or rather we came across – one of these until recently almost unknown pyramids on the afternoon of that first day in Cobá. And climbing it I was given, or saw, a second reason – a greater reason than its merely having a hotel at the end of the road – for thinking that this was the place I liked, I loved above all others in Mexico.

It wasn't just that the view, from the top of pyramid, was extraordinary; though it was, with storm clouds now starting to fill the great sky, the trees, as elsewhere, stretching away both up to and almost certainly way beyond the horizon, and the hillocks of other pyramids providing the only relief from the endless flatness. It wasn't even that the sheer scale and size of everything – of the sky and of the jungle – were so exhilarating as to make one feel intoxicated, despite the effort of climbing and, if one were me, the constant look out one felt one had to keep for anything that might be living amidst the stones. More, it was the combination of the view and the intoxication, with the illusion that such a place gives one, that here, now, just for this moment, one understands everything. One understands the world. One understands history. One understands one's own place in the world and in history; and one understands everyone else's, and everything else's, place. It is nonsense, of course, and one couldn't, if pressed, even explain precisely what one means. And yet one feels it. One tells oneself that one can see the pattern in everything, and see that everything, from the scorpion beneath one's feet, to the Spanish moss hanging off the topmost branches of the trees around one ('as if some troupe of witches had passed in the night and caught their shawls on them'), to the tiny figure standing on top of this pyramid, has a place in that pattern and is, inextricably, linked. And feeling it, however nonsensical it may be, one is happy; and for as long as one lives will probably think of the place where one felt it with affection, and will tell one's friends 'I loved it'.

We spent four days in Cobá, exploring the jungle, swimming, and reading about the Indians who inhabited or had inhabited the area. (The hotel, being French, had a library stacked with books about such matters. So one could have a 'vacance intelligente' if one were French, and if one were not, could mock and make use of it anyway.)

And then, in the middle of a rain-storm, confident that I now had the Maya and their past safely under my belt, and with an idea for a novel in the back of my mind, we left: to take the road back to Mérida and to undergo the last of my three little trials in the south.

We should have known that some further mishap was to befall us; because when we came out of the restaurant where we had stopped to have lunch, in a brief pause between the now almost continual storms, there was a vulture squatting on the roof of the car. Reason told one that it was trying to dry its feathers in the brief gaudy moment of sun; or at least planning to check up on the restaurant's garbage. But instinct said that it was warning one to beware. Somewhere along that empty road, the naked-necked beady-eyed creature seemed to be croaking, as very reluctantly it hobbled two paces forward along the metal before lifting off – to fly only as far as the gutter of the hotel, from where it could watch our departure – somewhere under these hectic clouds, you are going to enter *our* realm; and risk becoming our prey. So beware, beware – and farewell . . .

In fact, the bird was over pessimistic – or optimistic, depending on whose point of view one took – and nothing worse happened than, that night, somewhere between Can-Cun and Valladolid, the rain getting into the brakes of the car. Causing them to fail, and causing the vehicle, when we hit a bump, to skid off the road into a ditch. Even so – one should have taken more note of what instinct had said.

It was very dark. The rain was torrential. And when we got out, we realized that we couldn't move the car from the ditch by ourselves. We started to grope our way along the black highway, towards two flickering lights we saw in the far distance . . . And then, suddenly, as if from nowhere, a number of snarling dogs came bounding up to us. (Cousins of the vultures; or the vultures themselves, transformed.) I was only wearing shorts at the time, and had lost my shoes as I was scrambling out of the ditch; and at any moment, I thought, as I told myself keep walking, keep walking, and don't slow down or acknowledge in any way the presence of these hounds of hell (as, by now, they had become), they were going to sink their teeth into my calves and feet, and drag me into the grass by the roadside. So that by morning, when the vultures got their turn, I would already be half gone. And by the time some motorist saw me, and stopped, I would be as clean as a skeleton on display. With only one or two ants running around my skull, to make sure nothing had been missed.

Keep walking, I told myself. Keep walking.

But the dogs didn't bite; I was not dragged anywhere; and when a car went by, very fast, we saw in the headlights that though the animals were snapping and growling, they weren't doing so with much animosity, and their tails were wagging. And in fact the only real point of this story is that when we arrived at the flickering lights we had seen in the distance, and found they came from a small group of huts lit by hurricane lamps, it took us five minutes to explain what had happened, and ask for help. Because until someone who wasn't initially in the hut that we approached was called, none of the villagers spoke Spanish, or understood what Enrique was saying. And Enrique, though he knew one or two words of Nahautl, didn't speak a word of Maya.

Perhaps ten men accompanied us back through the torrential rain and gravely, and quietly, helped us to push and pull the car back on the road. And when they had done it they received our thanks with the same quiet gravity and went away, as if nothing unexpected had happened and they weren't at all disturbed at having been called out of their homes and soaked.

Either, I thought, they are used to people sliding off the road into ditches, or such stoicism and composure are part of their character.

Or possibly, I concluded – fantasy making one final appearance – they too, out in this empty, featureless land, are children and servants of the vultures; and had been sitting in their huts waiting for us to drive past. Knowing that we would drive past, but not knowing whether they would be called upon to help us continue on our way, or be summoned by their masters in the morning, to clear away the bones . . .

'But I'll tell you one thing,' I said to Gerardo as I came, in a slightly different form, to the end of my tale. 'I wish the same thing would happen to the man I met the other night. Then he'd see whether the Indians existed or not.'

I imitated the man's pretence at non-comprehension.

'Patronizing *fool*.'

*

'And after that?' Gerardo asked as we approached the museum where the Hockney exhibition was being held. 'What did you do then?'

'After the south, you mean? After we'd given the car back in Mérida?'

'Yes.'

'Oh after that,' I said, trying to remember what we had done. 'After that . . .'

We took a bus up through Tabasco, past the hurricane-flooded fields and the blackened stumps of trees, past the oil wells and the refineries and the smoking cities that smelled of sulphur and gas, and over grey fat rivers that had clumps of water weed floating in them. Water weed that seemed to have a life of its own, and would come heaving through the stream towards the ferries as if it were going to consume them.

It was on one of these ferries, shaped like a baking-tin, that we arrived in Ciudad del Carmen; a windswept sandy shabby island, where the hotel was filled with cowboy-hatted Texan oilmen, and where we had to pay three times over the odds to get a ferry-ticket off again.

'I don't care,' I said. 'I'd pay ten times over the odds to leave here.'

But it was just as well we did. Because the ferry we took off, the morning after our arrival, was the last for six days. Even as we were leaving 'el norte', the north wind, was getting up, making the crossing to the mainland uncomfortable. And once it was up – as we had been warned before – the island was entirely cut off.

'Can you imagine,' I said a week later, when I read in the paper that services had only just started again. 'We could have been there all this time.'

One would have been tempted to swim for it.

From Ciudad del Carmen we went to see the Olmec ceremonial site at La Venta, near Villahermosa, and the carved Olmec heads, over six foot high, which are on display there. And from there – it was on to Lake Catemaco.

But if this had been the birthplace of pre-Columbian culture, there was very little, now, to show for it. Just a small, melancholy, faintly middle-European resort; and, on the lake's edge, at the end of a long, dusty lane, a sprawling, practically empty hotel. Peeling, isolated and sad.

'You don't like the room?' the young woman behind the desk asked us, looking up from an old copy of *War and Peace*, as we returned to her office to tell her that indeed the chalet amidst the palms she had consigned to us wasn't to our liking. It was full of mosquitoes for one thing, and if the cockroach in the shower was dead, those in the bedroom were not. She waved her hand round at a board full of keys hanging on large wooden balls. 'Here,' she said, 'take your choice.' Then she returned to her book.

Maybe it was the lake, and the constant supply of fresh water that had inspired wandering Indians to make this place their home. Or maybe, even then, five thousand, ten thousand years ago, there had been this same melancholy atmosphere, and the wandering Indians had thought: this is far enough. Or maybe – maybe the comment that was made to me by a German woman was made by one Indian to another all that time ago; and he, like me, didn't know what else to do but agree.

I was sitting by a slapping, leaf-strewn swimming pool, looking out over the slapping, leaf-strewn lake. It was five o'clock in the afternoon, and all I could see, from where I sat, was the choppy grey-green surface of the water, and faintly, in the distance, the outline of the low surrounding hills. Hearing someone approach, and assuming it to be Enrique, I turned, and saw a stout, elderly and obviously German tourist, who must have been the only other guest. We smiled at each other and she went and leaned on the green, peeling railing of the parapet. She stared in the same direction I'd been staring in for some minutes, and appeared to find it as mournful, in its lovely way, as I had; for her reddish, solid though not unpleasant face looked suddenly – and un- usually, I suspect, for her – soft.

'Ist gut, no?' she said gently, nodding towards the lake, and smiling at me again.

What could I say?

'Ja,' I told her. 'Ist zehr gut.'

'Ist schön,' she sighed.

'Ja,' I repeated. 'Ist zehr schön.'

Zehr, zehr schön . . .

And so it was decided . . .

About Fortín de las Flores the only thing I can remember is that it was a faded misty hill-town; and that as if to prove that its reputation for the cultivation of gardenias was not unfounded, the swimming pool of the faded grand hotel where we stayed was filled with the things. Though they enhanced the sense of life being finished there, rather than doing anything to make the place more cheerful (or, like the hotel in Catemaco, more crowded). As did the many elderly immaculately-dressed waiters in the dining-room, standing around in the shadows waiting for guests who, almost certainly, were unlikely to arrive.

'Normally, you know, we do have other people staying here,' one felt those still, silent figures were trying to reassure one. 'As many as we did in the old days, when this place was first opened, and it was fashionable, and we were young. It's just today that you've happened on a quiet time . . .'

And about the train ride back into Mexico City – just that on it, I had my first experience of open hostility due, albeit mistakenly, to my race.

We had been on the train for some time; looking out of the windows at the slopes and nineteen thousand foot peak of Mount Orizaba, wondering how long the whole journey would take if we continued at this speed (answer: thirteen hours), and wonder- ing whether we should have brought any food other than the bananas we had purchased on Fortín station. I was, despite the heat and what I considered the likelihood of our toppling off the track and crashing down some ravine, enjoying myself; and Enrique was muttering that a bus would have covered the three hundred kilometres to Mexico City in a quarter of the time that this was going to take.

And then, as we sat there, a huge, fat, obviously drunk man came through the door at the end of the coach, looked around, spotted me, and coming straight to me, started shouting in my face.

If one cannot always rely on the kindness of strangers, one can generally rely on their indifference. When one cannot – panic sets in.

What had I done to annoy this bloated, greasy-haired giant, whose breath smelled of beer and whose shiny, brightly-coloured polyester shirt looked as if it were about to split open. Why me? What had I done?

Around me, I was aware of faces staring at the scene – though without a great deal of interest – and of Enrique, looking on and ready to intervene.

I turned to him, pressing back in my seat as the oaf repeated what he had said, only shouting it louder this time. I felt as if the floor of the carriage were cracking beneath me.

'What,' I said to Enrique, 'does he *want*?'

Enrique nodded at me, and instead of answering, leaned towards the man.

'No es nortamericano,' he said. 'Es inglés.'

The transformation couldn't have been more sudden or more complete. Even as he was preparing to shout at me again the giant's scowl turned into a grin. Even as he looked as if he were going to hit me the clenched fist turned into a slap on the shoulder. And even as some obviously indefensible sin was going to be thrown in my face, the expression of accusal turned to one of almost parodied regret. I wasn't American? I was English? The giant seemed about to weep as he grinned. The slap on the shoulder turned into a clasp on both shoulders. I was lifted right out of my seat and hugged. And then, as I was dropped again, and my hand was now grabbed and shaken up and down, I was invited to come with him and have a drink. Beer, whisky, brandy, tequila. You name it. You must come, he said. Please. He was so sorry. English, not American. English – well yes, of course, now I said so, he could see. Oh God he was sorry – so , so sorry. I must come and have a drink with him. Please. Beer, whisky – whatever I liked. Please. *Please.*

I am not a brave person, and will generally do whatever I can to avoid trouble.

Nevertheless, I did pluck up enough courage to say, I hoped grandly, 'No' and to pick up my book again and pretend to start reading. And even when I did of course weaken sufficiently to glance up nervously, give my own apologetic smile now, and add 'Thank you,' it wasn't, I also hoped, too abject a step back. 'Go and have a drink with you after what you've just said,' I wanted to tell him – 'you must be mad.'

Besides, I wouldn't have gone to have a drink with you anyway. Fat, drunken . . .

As if the man could read my thoughts – and wasn't, luckily, too offended by them – he muttered something else, almost whispering in his effort to prove how sincere his apologies were.

'What,' I muttered sideways to Enrique, 'does he want now?'

'He only wants to know,' Enrique said, 'if he can look at your ticket.'

'My ticket?'

'Yes,' he nodded, as he produced his own from his pocket. 'You see – he's the ticket collector.'

*

'And that,' I said to Gerardo, 'was that.'

We got into Mexico City station at eleven o'clock that night, and three days later, I left.

FIFTEEN

On Art And Artists (II)

Despite my determination to compare David Hockney favourably with his Mexican fellow artists, in fact little need be said on the subject of 'El Gran Teatro di David Hockney' (an exhibition mainly of theatrical and operatic designs) except that it was somewhat disappointing; the sets and costumes lacking spirit out of their proper context, and the few paintings, lithographs and photo-montages on display looking – to eyes that were growing accustomed to Mexican ripeness? – a little thin, shallow and meretricious. And – that I would have been ashamed of my earlier thoughts about wit and irony had there not been, in the final room, a number of paintings by the artist after whom the museum had been named; 'Mexico's greatest living artist: Rufino Tamayo.' As it was, seeing these last, soft, sentimental canvases, one felt that everything one had seen before, even if not up to one's hopes and expectations, had been masterly; and one had no option *but* to compare Hockney favourably – with Tamayo if with no one else.

And on the subject of Tamayo himself even less need be said; except that to my eyes his work provided further evidence of the dangers that Mexico put in the way of persons of European descent. ('On the one hand it makes them dissatisfied with so-called wit, irony, and spirit, while on the other it does nothing to prepare them for the nourishment it can provide; nourishment that the European trained stomach is culturally, historically, maybe even physically unable to digest. So that they are tempted to seek substance in the mere appearance of flowers, the mere surface of the – admittedly lovely – earth; and to risk renouncing the spirit without ever, really, having any possibility of living comfortably in the flesh.

Put it this way: Rufino Tamayo falls between two stools; and thinks he provides a bridge between the two.')

But on the subject of the third – and the last – of the artists whose work I looked at in my week of waiting – a good deal needs be said. Or is going to be, even if it doesn't.

In one of the interviews with Hockney in the Mexico City press – and there had been many – he had said that among the things he wanted to do while in town for the opening of his show was visit Frida Kahlo's house. And everyone I knew had told me the same. 'You must go to Frida Kahlo's house. You must go to Frida Kahlo's.'

So, the day after my disappointment with the English painter – and my dismissal of the Mexican – I set off for Coyoacan; both because I wanted to anyway, and in the hope of seeing something better than I had already seen.

Perhaps the woman, I told myself, will succeed where the men failed. And even if she doesn't, at least Coyoacan – a fashion-able suburb in the south of the city, popular with well-heeled bohemians and foreigners – is pleasant to walk in.

To tell the truth, until about three months before I had hardly heard of Frida Kahlo, and only became aware of her then because I bought a book with her self-portrait on the cover. But once I had arrived, and people started telling me I should go to see her house, I learned the following facts about her. She was born in 1910. She was Diego Rivera's second wife. She was a painter herself. And she died in 1954. She had also, books said – hoping to tantalize – led a 'tragic, tormented life.'

However, until I had seen her paintings I wasn't sure if I was interested in her tragedy or her torment. Besides, I thought, if that description isn't just romantic hyperbole, it is very likely that whatever problems she had will be evident in her work itself; which will make any further reading unnecessary.

And in this I was not wrong; what must have been the principal problem of Frida Kahlo's life *was* evident in her work. And any other problems she had must have stemmed from this one central problem.

It was this. That Frida Kahlo, as far as one can judge, had no talent. Not one scrap. There was no 'divine spark' in her; neither when she was at the start of her career, nor when she reached her maturity, nor at the time of her early death. And yet because she was Rivera's wife, and only because she was Rivera's wife, she was able to set herself up as a painter, foist her still-born offerings upon the public, and leave her house, and its contents, to the world. To a world which would troop around that house nodding at efforts that would make the most amateur Sunday painter look inspired. To a world that would be intimidated by the busts, portraits, statues and photographs of Stalin which, aptly, dominate it. And to a world that would be bamboozled into believing that these badly drawn, ugly-coloured, faux-naif pictures that don't even attain sentimentality, were a testament to one woman's struggle to live honestly; to an *artist's* struggle to live honestly.

If I were a woman I should be incensed that such a person, whose only real claim to fame was that she married a famous man, should be taken seriously; let alone as an artist of a certain importance. As incensed as I should be if a woman who could only sing out of tune in a tiny, ugly, inexpressive voice expected the world to take her seriously simply because she was married to a great tenor. She is a traitor, I would think; a turncoat, a charlatan, a cheat.

As it was – I simply walked out of the house after fifteen minutes, and went, feeling depressed, down to the Viveros; a park that was a cross between a botanical garden and a flower market. At least there was an exhibition of azaleas . . .

Garbage, I muttered to myself, thinking back at what I had just seen, as I passed banks of white flowers. Lying, hateful nonsense; as I passed banks of yellow, and orange, and red. And insulting, patronizing, contemptuous and contemptible rubbish; as I passed the pink. 'How *can* people think her any good?' But by the time I had got to the blue, which I had never seen before, the refrain was merely 'Oh well, it was undoubtedly she who paid most highly for her sin, and maybe that's the lesson to be learned from that museum: that if you're wicked there's a good chance you will pay for it one way or another.' And by the time I left, going out past a final display of multi-coloured azaleas, an explosion of blossoms, I wasn't even feeling depressed any longer. 'Oh hell,' I was telling myself, very much as I had on the train to Oaxaca, all those years ago, 'Who cares about wickedness and sin? When there are flowers like this to be seen . . .'

*

A postscript.

Although I had cooled down by the time I left the Viveros, I spent the rest of that day feeling fairly indignant. So when, at six o'clock, I met Georgina, I first of all made a speech denouncing Frida Kahlo as a dishonest woman, and then, when we went out to have a drink with a French writer friend of hers, who had published a book that day, I made another speech denouncing Frida Kahlo as a dishonest painter.

'Although even that's to praise her too highly. Because she simply wasn't a painter. Just – dishonest.'

I must have gone on for a good half hour; glad that I had a chance to get everything off my chest, and had an audience who didn't seem to mind my running on in this fashion. I said how suitable it was that Stalin should be the patron saint of that house, with its folk costumes and Frida's collection of particularly crude pre-Columbian statuettes alongside the paintings; for only a tyrant such as Stalin would be able to justify such dishonesty, and only a tyrant such as Stalin would still have the power, even after all these years, to make people continue to take Frida Kahlo seriously. I said that the only thing she seemed to have learned from her husband – who compared to her, looks like a very great painter – was that if you wanted to do paintings for 'the people' you had to represent 'the people' in those paintings as poor ignorant ugly fools. Which almost guaranteed that only those who thought that 'the people' were poor, ignorant, ugly fools would ever want to look at them. The poor, ignorant, ugly fools themselves, I added, rather than be spat at in this fashion, would rather spend two hours watching Hollywood's version of life, which told them 'You'll never be like this, but it's not going to do you too much harm fantasising that you might be, once or twice a week.' Or would prefer to sit in a church for an hour or two a week and, amidst swirling altars, tortured Christs, and wild gold, hear God tell them that while He knows as well as they know themselves that they are poor, ignorant, ugly fools, He loves them nevertheless, and that they have a place in this world as much as anyone else and certainly quite as much as certain thick eye-browed intellectuals. And finally I said, getting warmed up to my subject, that while I didn't actually believe in God myself, it seemed to me that the only way a painter (or a writer, I meant but didn't say) could ever hope to paint anything 'true', anything 'real', and at the same time, save him or herself from being *only* a buffoon of the powerful, was if he/she were to offer his/her work to whatever it was that people who did believe in God meant by that word God. 'Perhaps not consciously. In fact almost definitely not consciously.' But only if they did that, I concluded, did they have any chance of achieving, let's say, greatness; or of tweaking, whether they meant to or not, the Duke of Mantua's beard.

Or rocking the bust of Stalin?

That was what I meant by painters having a divine spark. That was what Rivera and company turned their back on and Frida Kahlo lacked altogether. And that, I supposed – and really to expose myself at the last – was what there seemed to me to be a great strain of in certain parts of Mexican society, and in certain parts of the Mexican character: an unwillingness, or an inability, to believe in, or accept the concept of what was generally meant by 'God'. The reasons for this were undoubtedly many – historical, geographical, climactical. But even from the beginning, while there had always been a willingness to believe in *gods*, (and later, as the great civilizations declined, an increasing willingness to believe in magic), to believe in one all-powerful *God* – no. Or less and less, as time went by. And finding themselves unable to be consoled or convinced by any one God, the Indians had tried to fill the emptiness they felt with practical day-to-day affairs, with that increasing reliance on magic – and drugs – and, both literally and figuratively, with flowers.

It was the strain of godlessness in Mexican culture that was at the root of the danger that Mexico presented to those of European descent. And it was the strain of godlessness which tempted them to look back to the god whom their fellow Europeans to the north and across the Atlantic worshipped; the god, with a small g, that they could never quite reconcile with the God with a capital G. The god who was the heir to Quetzalcoatl, who claimed to be the god of civilization, and who would have one forget what he had done, what he had had to do, in order to secure that civilization.

The fair god . . .

At which point I stopped, shook my head, and, though not really feeling embarrassed, apologized to Georgina, her French writer friend, and another mutual friend of theirs, for having so carried on.

'What a way,' I said to the writer, 'to spend your publication day. Listening to me sounding off.'

'That's all right,' said Olivier, and smiled.

'Anyway,' I went on, 'good luck, here's to success, and . . .' I stopped. 'By the way, what's the book about?'

There was a pause as Olivier exchanged glances with the two girls. Then they all three grinned.

'*I'm* sorry now,' he said, looking back at me.

'Why?'

'Can't you guess?'

I started to feel uncomfortable.

'No,' I said. 'I've no idea.'

'Well what do you *think* the book's about?'

'I don't know. Unless . . .' I paused, and blushed. 'Not . . .'

'Yes,' Olivier smiled. 'Of course. What else?'

What else indeed.

'Oh God,' I said. 'Forgive me.'

Rivera, and Frida Kahlo . . .

SIXTEEN

Two Bad Days

Of my wasted day I wrote the following in my diary:

'A grey day.

I walked around the city. I went into some bookshops. But I learned nothing, I did nothing, and by the evening felt I had been lugging myself around like a heavy suitcase; a suitcase I couldn't put down. I was stuck with me, and I was bored with me, and to make matters worse, I thought I had a cold coming on and took an aspirin, which made me feel woolly-headed, and bleary.

Eventually I came home and tried to write. But all I could manage were show-stopping sentences like "Only by loving can we save ourselves from the past", or "Only by loving can we achieve reality"; sentences which, while probably true, didn't really get me very far.

Because for the life of me I couldn't see how I could relate such grand statements to Mexico, or my being here.

Though maybe, I thought . . .

Luckily, I was saved from further speculation – and further writing – by José arriving with a gang of relatives: aunts, cousins, nephews, nieces. And by the time I had finished explaining who I was and what I was doing, and they had all finished drinking coffee and eating cakes, it was too late to do anything except say goodnight, go to bed, and sleep.

So I did, and woke this morning feeling more cheerful.

The sun is shining.'

And of the day after – this:

'I came out of the P's house to hear a thin, mean English voice saying "No, no *leave* it", and to see a thin, mean English man shooing away a weary-looking Mexican from a piece of electrical equipment. A film crew was setting up a chase sequence in the quiet residential street for what appeared to be an Anglo-American movie – the director being someone who lives just one street away from me in London – and Mexico was clearly getting to this second or third assistant-something. There was panic in his pinched petulant mouth, panic in his pale, accusing eyes. And one could tell that he hated it here as much as the artists in San Miguel hated it there; surrounded by all these brown people. And one could hear, already, what he would say of the place once he had left it. Something about it being uncivilized, Third World, dirty.

A man, I mentally noted, without any flowers in his soul.

*

In the evening I went to the theatre with Eugenia and Fernando and two friends to see a Dario Fo play, *Accidental Death of an Anarchist*. The dramatic equivalent of a Rivera painting: populist, patronizing, and crude. The audience for this supposedly up-roarious comedy denouncing the bourgeoisie was composed, predictably, of the golden-haired children of the bourgeoisie, a number of bearded and dishevelled caricatures of intellectuals, and one or two (what looked like) Mexican or Chilean professors; whose laughter, unlike that of the golden hairs and the beards, arrived always a second late. It was accompanied by a knowing nod and the self-satisfied air that comes from *understanding* what one is laughing at. And hearing those self-conscious, over-loud brays, and seeing those young men and women in their well-cut jeans and silk shirts, and those older men in suits, I not only wished that I wasn't where I was, but couldn't help reflecting that all in all – this has been a fairly wretched week.

It's time to be off again.

It certainly was, and it certainly had been. But then, on the Monday, the day before I did set off again, something unexpected happened; something that, at the last moment, almost redeemed the whole week.

Magic!

Whatever else it did, it sent me off, on Tuesday morning, feeling sure I was going to enjoy my second trip with Georgina.

SEVENTEEN

An Epilogue

Monday, March 10

When I went out this morning to buy my paper the old flower woman was back on the grass verge opposite the school, with a fresh mass of carnations, roses and irises to sort through. I took a good look at her. She couldn't be the same one as before, I thought. That one died. I'm sure she was dead. She *looked* dead.

But she was the same one, so I must have been mistaken, and my poetic tragedy hadn't been a tragedy at all.

Hell, I told myself, as I continued on my way. That's a nice little story spoiled.

Unless, I went on, unless – she either did die and has come back to life, or she doesn't actually exist at all, but is just a ghost; some sort of symbolic figure, sitting in the grass looking at the fine young things over the way. Reminding them that they too must fade; and that they mustn't waste their brief and glorious bloom. Memento mori . . .

Coming back from Sanborns I must have been so carried away by my fantasy that I stared too long at the old woman as I passed her. For without in the least changing her expression she raised a hand and offered me a wilting red carnation.

Memento mori . . .

'No gracias señora,' I said, refusing her offer and walking on.

Not today, thank you.

EIGHTEEN

On The Road Again

For all my confidence that I was going to enjoy myself, to begin with it seemed that my second journey was going to start no better than my first. Georgina, when we left, was not in a good mood. She had had an argument with her former boss at the television; her mother, having been a widow for many years, had suddenly married again and gone to live in the States ('I don't know which I mind more. It's ridiculous, I know, to mind either. But I do.'); and, what seemed to irritate her most, the weather report for the area we were going to was not good. Wind, rain, and unseasonably low temperatures were forecast.

'And I wanted to swim,' Georgina groused as we sat in a traffic jam, and I persuaded her that with the forecast as bad as it was there was no point in her making a trip half-way across town to go to a particular shop she liked to buy a pair of shorts. 'I mean that's all I *came* for. I'm not interested in pyramids or cities or land-scapes. I've never been to Vera Cruz and I've never wanted to go to Vera Cruz. It's just the *sun* I want, and the sea.' She changed gear, and we shot through a light that had just turned red. 'And even at the best of times everyone's always told me that the gulf is pretty ugly.'

When we got out of the city, we took the road to the north-east, past the pyramids at Teotihuacán; a road which, though in no way green and lush like that through the mountains to the south, was a good deal more attractive than the road due north, to Querétaro. But even there things did not improve very much: since first we couldn't find a gas station, and then, when we left the highway to look for one, we got lost.

'This is ridiculous,' Georgina snapped, as she put the car into reverse, and we hurtled backwards, in the hope that the turn-off we had just passed was the one we had wanted. (It wasn't.) And 'I really don't know why I'm doing this,' as we did finally find the route back to the highway, and realized we had been going round in circles. 'I've got no money, I've got no job, and I'm going where I don't want to go.'

But then, once we got further away from the city, and the sky, against all predictions, got bluer instead of cloudier, Georgina relaxed, and decided that after all she was glad she had come, and that since she was going to start working again full time in April she might just as well get out of town while she had the opportunity.

'It's just such an *effort* leaving the city,' she sighed, as she slowed down to a reasonable hundred and ten kilometres an hour and assured me that for the rest of the trip she would go no faster. 'And my mother's getting married again *has* upset me, even though I know it's absurd. I suppose it's because I'm an only child, and I liked to think of her as mine in a way.'

I nodded sympathetically, and asked what her father had died of.

'My father?' Georgina echoed. 'Oh –' as if it were one of the commonest causes of death '– he was murdered. A man who was working for him shot him.'

And after that everything went well. The landscape slowly changed from parched, flat, mainly yellow-brown high plains to an Alpine, rather Swiss-looking scene – all tall pines, still lakes, bright sun flickering through the trees, and an air that, despite the sun, became so cold that we had to close the windows. Georgina's mood, as we climbed and climbed, improved apace; until, as she stopped the car, we got out, and she spread her arms in the air as if about to sing to the valleys and the further mountains peeling away beneath, she could say, with a laugh, 'We not just are high, but I feel high.' And I, who had started to be afraid that not only was this trip not going to be enjoyable, but was going to be a disaster, and also that I was going to have to make a constant effort to stop it becoming worse, felt relaxed enough to say 'Thank God', and to tell Georgina of what I'd been afraid.

'I mean I don't mind being nice to you for a while. But for the whole trip?'

Indeed so far up did we go, that though we eventually had to come down – and as we came down, and the air started to smell thick, and heavy, and tropical, the weather began to do what we had heard it would do – we managed to remain feeling fairly high.

And neither the low grey clouds, nor the shacks we drove past with barefooted women and children standing in the muddy doorways staring at the falling rain, nor Papantla ('the centre of Mexico's vanilla industry, where the Indians swing round a type of maypole with their feet attached to ribbons'), really managed to bring us back to earth.

Though that was, so far as Papantla was concerned, just as well. For Papantla was not an attractive place; and had we not still been in a reasonably good mood when we arrived, we might well have ended up feeling truly miserable.

First of all, the only hotel we could find, while large, and in the centre of town, was cold and shabby and damp. Broken tiles made its would-be moorish design look tawdry; and a used Kleenex on the floor of the first room the manager showed us made us understand why the man's smile, as he shrugged and backed out of the room, was so wistful.

'You're not really going to like it here,' his eyes and his lips seemed to say. 'How could you? But on the other hand, staying here – if only for one night – you will understand what we have to put up with, always.'

Then, always a bad sign in a Mexican town – the only other place where it happened being San Miguel – we couldn't find a bar where we could have a beer. Something Georgina needed after her day of driving; and I needed after a quick tepid shower that had involved washing myself while looking up at the shower head, across at the window which wouldn't quite close, and down at the sinister drain, wondering what, at any moment, was going to appear through them.

And finally, when, after much asking and shaking of heads, ('A beer?' with an expression of wonder. 'In *this* place'), we were directed through a scratched broken door, across a dank, garbage-strewn courtyard, up a urine-smelling and graffiti-scrawled staircase, and into an empty pool hall with an only half-illuminated counter at one end and a deserted terrace-café down one side, we found that the terrace was looking out over the main square, and that at any moment a local pop singing contest was going to start.

Two minutes later – after a woman had come up to our table and asked us, as if she couldn't imagine what we were doing there, if we wanted something – it did. Loud, harsh, insistent, by men who were too old and fat for their suits, or by children who were too young and small to hold their guitars, the songs were belted out through the humid, none too warm night; causing invisible crows and starlings to squawk in the trees, a faintly curious though not very interested crowd to gather slowly round the stage that had been erected for the occasion, and one or two people to take refuge in the pool hall. People who every now and then drifted out onto the terrace, looked down, and sighed.

'And yet,' I said to Georgina, as the crowd below clapped politely and without enthusiasm, 'it's still not as bad – not half as bad – as San Miguel. I mean I would hang *myself* from my feet if I had to live here, and swing *myself* round maypoles. But even so – in its down at heel way – it has a sort of charm. After all – there's no atmosphere of menace, or hostility, or even misery here. And maybe if we weren't tired, and it hadn't been raining, and it were a little warmer . . .'

Georgina gave me a look as if to say 'Who are you fooling?' And then she raised her hand in the hope that someone would see it and bring us something to eat, and smiled. 'What this town needs,' she said, 'is a bomb.'

Though even she, after a second beer and a hamburger, was prepaired to admit that Papantla wasn't *that* bad. Bad enough, and another of those places she never wanted to see again. Even so – yes, she agreed. It *wasn't* as bad as San Miguel.

At least there were no artists here.

*

There weren't any tourists either. Which was odd, since aside from its commercial importance as the vanilla capital of Mexico, it was the nearest town to El Tajin; an Olmec and Totonac ceremonial site I had long wanted to see, and was in fact the reason we had come to Papantla.

There weren't even any French around; 'which must be some sort of first.'

And not only in Papantla, but also, the following morning, when we drove out to El Tajin, at the site itself. Apart from a ticket seller, one or two stall-holders selling soft drinks, and an archaeologist and his assistant who I thought might be French but turned out on closer inspection not to be, the place was as deserted as most other things in this area seemed to be. There was just the still, grey, heavy rain-threatening sky and – from one moment to the next – the heavy, also somehow grey, tropical heat. There was just the smell of hot, heavy vegetation, and the quiet, broken every now and then by a shriek or a whistle, from the surrounding jungle-covered hills. And there was just the pyramid and the other remaining buildings; ornate, in the middle of nowhere and, though impeccably kept, unvisited.

We wandered round in a sort of listless daze for an hour or two. Then, wondering why we felt as awed as we did – the setting, the silence, the stones? – we drifted back towards the car. A small barefooted child approached us, appearing out of nowhere, wanting to sell us some locally made drums. I shook my head and smiled, and Georgina said softly 'No niño, no.'

A group of Indians, wearing traditional white cotton costumes that tied tight around the ankles – to protect themselves from the small burrowing insects which infest the area – had materialized, and were clearing the grass round the car-park; talking amongst themselves in, we assumed, Totonac.

A man stood watching us from the entrance to a wooden hut above which was written simply 'El Tajin'.

The morning was so still that when I spoke to Georgina I lowered my voice.

'Shall we,' I said, nodding towards the wooden hut, 'go in there?'

Georgina nodded.

'We might as well, now we're here.'

I don't know what we expected to find.

In fact, apart from a rack of shelves in the centre of the hut, on which there were a few dusty sets of postcards, and another shelf running down one wall, the place was practically empty. But what made it less than completely empty – and what made me go over, and stare – was what was contained in a series of bigger or smaller glass pickling jars on the shelf that ran down the length of the wall.

'There you see,' I said to Georgina. 'I'm right to think this country's dangerous. If I'd known these were here . . .'

The pickling jars contained, a notice informed one, just some of the creatures that had been found on the site, and were native to this zone. On the left, in the way of centipedes, spiders, and largish, swollen snakes, curled up and looking as if they were asleep in their preserving liquid, were what were labelled as the merely 'very poisonous' species. And on the right, in the way of five very small dead snakes, were what were labelled as the 'fatal'.

'Do not, under any circumstances, pick up stones or wander off the beaten track,' the notice concluded. '¡PELIGRO!'

'The way I feel about life,' I said.

'Though I must say it's just as well we didn't come in here before going round, otherwise I might not have.'

Feeling that I had cheated the gods yet again, I got back in the car, and we drove off.

'Oh don't be ridiculous,' Georgina said, uncertain whether I was joking or not. 'That's what you're supposed to feel. That's why they put those bottles there. I bet they haven't actually seen a snake round here for years.'

'Maybe not. But – you never know, do you? I mean – you only need one . . .'

*

The rest of that morning was spent by both of us trying to work out what the sweet, sharp, almost peppery smell of insecticide was that we had noticed yesterday coming down from the mountains and noticed again now every so often; spent by me looking out at the passing landscape so I could fix it in my memory and later, when we stopped at some hotel, write it down; and spent by me once again, though at Georgina's instigation this time, trying to do something about the weather; which, the nearer we got to the coast, became more and more gloomy.

'Don't worry,' I said, having calculated that if we kept going at the same speed we would reach the sea around two, 'At two, on the dot, the sun will come out. You'll see.'

Georgina took her eyes off the road for a moment, and nodded at me. 'Yes,' she said. 'I'll see.'

'You think I'm joking, don't you? But I'm not. At two o'clock – on the dot.'

Georgina nodded again, and we drove on.

'I know what it is,' she said some time later, as once more the smell of insecticide hit us; so strong this time that it caught at the back of our throats. 'It isn't insecticide at all. It's oranges, and tangerines. See.'

Looking out at the green densely-leaved trees growing on either side of the road, that were as hung with fruit as an overdecorated Christmas tree with baubles, I sniffed and wondered if she were right. 'You mean they spray them with insecticide?'

'No. That is, they may. They probably do. But that isn't the insecticide you can smell. That's the orange trees themselves. I knew it reminded me of something. My mother has an orange tree at home.'

'*Had*.'

'*Had* an orange tree at home. And that's the smell exactly. Only at home of course there is – was – only one. Whereas here . . .'

Here, at times, they stretched away for miles.

'How strange,' I said, as, now that the smell had been identified, I not only realized that Georgina was right, but felt that it was even more overpowering and unpleasant than before. 'Maybe it's some natural insecticide that orange trees have. Or maybe commercial insecticides have that smell put in them as a perfume. But I do know one thing. Any time now I want to bring back the gulf of Mexico – I shall just give a squirt of Flit or something – and breathe in deeply.'

'I must remember this,' I added a little later, 'for my notes.'

That – and the fact that though the word 'tropical' conjures up, at least in northern minds, images of things wild and overgrown and overblown, like a Rousseau painting come to life, when one is actually going through 'the tropics' one's most frequent reaction is not 'How extraordinary, how exotic,' but 'How, after all, very much like home this is.'

'Constable country,' I wrote. 'With palms and Spanish moss. And egrets in the grass around the lowing cows.'

'Look,' I said to Georgina, as the very symbol of Mexico rose out of a field to our right. 'An eagle, with a snake caught in its talons.'

'Look,' I said to Georgina, as, from the middle of another field, a flame rose into the air. 'A magic fire.'

(It was natural gas burning off; we had reached oil country.)

And 'Look,' I said to Georgina, as the vegetation became sparser and more coastal, and my watch showed ten minutes to two. 'The clouds are starting to break.'

At two o'clock exactly – after we had left the car outside an empty restaurant where the bamboo roof was half blown away, the tin tables were corroded by the salt, and the owner, sweeping the sand from the damp cement floor, said mournfully 'You don't want to eat, do you?', after we had walked down across the huge desolate beach whose only other occupants were a group of students standing around an old Volkswagen, and a man who was paddling at the grey-green water's edge, and after Georgina had looked up and said 'Well, maybe,' – at two o'clock exactly, the sun came out.

And within minutes, there wasn't a cloud in the sky.

'You see,' I said. 'I'm a magician.'

*

The long straight pot-holed road to the south, on which Georgina was scared of breaking an axle.

('Poor Mexico. When we can't even repair our roads.'

'They may be bad here. But they're worse in New York City.'

'Oh come now, you're joking.'

'Oh no,' I said, 'I'm not.')

The white, peeling, guestless hotels, with their palms all bent away from the sea as if in horror, and their empty restaurants with frayed bamboo roofs, corroded tables, and sandy, damp, cemented floors.

('You're lucky to find this weather now. It's the first sun we've seen in weeks. Just the *norte* blowing all the time. It's the worst early spring I can remember.' A pause. 'You don't want to eat, do you?'

'You *do*?')

And the landscape slowly, slowly changing, from almost England to something far more mountainous and wild.

('Have you noticed that further north there were mostly crows? But here it's more buzzards – and hawks – and vultures.')

*

I had been warned that the city of Vera Cruz was grey and ugly and very hot. But I found it white, attractive in its large sea-port way, and while quite hot, no hotter than it needed to be to keep Georgina happy.

We spent some time there exploring, visiting a painter friend of Eugenia's, making an occasional visit to one of the crowded, not unpleasant, but slightly run-down beaches. ('Obviously all these people living here must come all the time. But it's as if they're not really accustomed to relaxation, to leisure. There's something anxious about them. As if they want to have a good time, and know – have been told – that when they're on the beach they should have a good time. But for one reason or another – they can't quite manage it.') And yet, like Guanajuato, like Querétaro, like Guadalajara, enjoy it though I did, I found it didn't really make an impression on me as San Miguel de Allende or Frida Kahlo's house in Coyoacan had done; and made me reflect that if I were good at either I was better at condemning than praising; and in any case, even if I weren't, I preferred it. For while I was happy in Vera Cruz, and while, too, I had found the previous week in Mexico City dispiriting, having spent almost all my time attacking someone or something, I was no more than happy here; and thus felt myself becoming duller, dimmer, less perceptive. Whereas if I had hated it, or been apprehensive about it – like an animal that catches the scent of blood or an enemy on the wind – all my senses would have been put on the alert, and I would have come back with pages and pages of notes. Evidence for the prosecution.

And so, with one exception, it went on, for the rest of the journey; all my nerve-endings being massaged, all my fears being allayed with that constant whisper: 'Relax'. And even when we did, towards the end of our travels, go to a place that made a deep impression on me, I was certain that had I hated it, it would have made a deeper one. But I didn't hate Xalapa at all; I couldn't. Not a place that confirmed almost every one of my theories and prejudices about Mexico.

Xalapa is a high, generally wet and enormously fertile town up in the mountains some three hours out of the city of Vera Cruz; the capital of the state of Vera Cruz, and the site, I had been told, of one of the best universities in Mexico. And whether it was the contrast of arriving from the hot tropical coast into this cool, misty mountain town, that was being trailed over by curtains of rain when we reached it late one afternoon, whether it was that, being the state capital, it felt itself more important than the other towns we had visited, or whether it was the presence of the university and thus of its students, as soon as we had reached it, we could almost smell, in the fresh chilly air, that this place was different.

And not only smell, but see. There were bookstalls under the arcades that lined the main streets. There were posters advertising concerts and plays, and dance recitals. There were exhibitions of photographs and drawings. And above all, there was a shine in the eyes of the inhabitants, a sense of purpose in their faces, that made one feel one had stumbled not just into a new town, but into a new country altogether. As if, up here among the clouds, we had left the physical plain behind, and ascended to a city of the spirit.

It was invigorating; it made one feel light-headed; and despite the rain it made Georgina and I, once we had found a hotel, leave the car and wander round as though in a dream.

'Of course it's only the altitude,' I said as we walked through the now dark, shiny, cobbled streets, where not a beggar was to be seen, and where everyone, except us, seemed to be going somewhere. 'Or at any rate the difference in temperature.'

Nevertheless – one felt it – *we* felt it – and whatever the reason, we continued to feel it as we wandered in and out of galleries, spent what seemed like hours picking through the books on the stalls, and ended up on the deserted terrace of a café, overlooking the valley below.

'Where the red and white tin umbrellas, bent every which way like the palms on the coast road, dripped constantly onto the white tin tables and the chairs, tipped forward against them; and where, from far away, somewhere out there, down there in the night, the hoot of a train could be heard. Hoo, hoo, hoo – echoing through the darkness. As if it were lonely, and looking for a mate.'

And that it wasn't entirely an imaginary feeling was proved, to my satisfaction, by what we saw when, cold, wet-footed, and tired at last, we decided to make our way back to the hotel before going to see a movie. Getting lost, we came to the main square; which we'd been looking for before but hadn't found. And there, on one side of it, was the town's cathedral.

It wasn't a particularly attractive building from the outside, and it wasn't a particularly attractive building inside either. Yet it's attractiveness wasn't really the point. What was the point – or so it seemed to me – was that the church was not at all 'typically Mexican'. There was none of the ornateness, the wildness, the *floweriness* that one – rightly – associates with most Mexican church architecture. There was no trace of the baroque. Instead, if incompletely, if more in intent than in realization, the cathedral at Xalapa was gothic.

High, vaulted, soaring – it made one feel that it was reaching for the spirit, wanting to go beyond the body, stretching up towards some sort of safety.

It made one feel that one were suddenly in the North.

*

One other thing occurred in Xalapa to remind me – to reassure me that I was right to think – that Mexico is, on the whole, the country of the flower and not the dream, of the real and not the ideal. And it wasn't the film that Georgina and I went to see that night; although since it was an American remake of a Brazilian original (and while the Brazilian original was the better film, the American remake, being more polished, more professional, more illusory, ended by making one feel, paradoxically, that it was more real than the model on which it was based) I did try to make out that this too was an illustration of my point.

'You see it's the *illusion* of reality that convinces, not the attempt to reproduce reality. It's the *dream* of reality that satisfies, not the attempted representation of the thing itself. That's why the Americans, who are idealistic, are so good at making films, and why other people – who are less so, or not at all – are good only at making "art movies". The Americans understand that the truth lies in the dream, and that "reality" – by which those other people mean the appearance of reality – is, perhaps, only an illusion itself. Indeed, one could go so far as to say that in a film, appearance is always, only, has to be, an illusion.'

No, the other thing that made me confident that my way of looking at Mexico, while undoubtedly not the only way, wasn't entirely a wrong way, was the visit that we made the following morning to the museum in Xalapa. It was a bright fresh magnificent morning, with the air so clear and the view so sharp, after the rain, that one felt almost sea-sick; as if one were being rocked about in a boat amidst huge, tree-covered Alpine waves. And as we made our way across the cut, glistening grass of the museum grounds, in which stood more of the great Olmec heads I had seen four years before at La Venta, I felt, if only slightly, apprehensive. For the museum in Xalapa houses the biggest and the best collection of Olmec and Totonac art in the whole of Mexico.

'That would really mess me up,' I told Georgina, 'if I found I didn't like them at all now. All my ideas about the Olmecs being not only the first of the civilizations of Mexico, but also the only one apparently to have any idealism in their culture . . .'

All my ideas about the other, later civilizations; whose lack of idealism ensured that, while their members were clearly very practical – great architects, great potters, great astronomers, great mathematicians – they would not develop as, across the sea, the Europeans would develop; and would, thus, one day be overrun by those Europeans. Undone by their lack of development, undone by their acceptance of the myth of the returning Quetzalcoatl. But undone above all by their failure to dream; and so have the power, the ruthlessness, the vision to drive out the invaders, and repel them with a god of their own.

I need not have worried however; and far from being a disappointment, my second and more thorough contact with the Olmecs was even more rewarding than my first. Statues, figurines, the paintings on the vases – all of them spoke of some sort of a refinement, some sort of attempt to reach, through the individual, the universal. And seeing them, I became more than ever sure that in this – admittedly small – measure of idealism that the Olmecs possessed, and in the almost complete absence of it that all their successors possessed, lay the key not only to the creation of the first American civilization, but to the whole history of Mexico, up to the present day.

'For the Olmecs,' I wrote in my diary that evening, 'alone of the pre-Columbian cultures, appear to have had some concept of "God", rather than gods. They alone appear to have had some vision, or struggled towards some vision, of life in its totality; of the world, and everything in it, being not just united, but one. Having this vision, they conferred upon themselves a sense of their own reality; a reality that can still be seen in their sculptures. Lacking this vision, or failing to struggle further towards it, those who came after the Olmecs condemned themselves to a lack of growth; to a gradual loss of their sense of reality; and to eventual defeat.

All those who fail to struggle towards "God" – which struggle we call love – condemn themselves to a sense of unreality . . .'

The following morning we left for Puebla, and, after a short stay there, for home.

NINETEEN

Farewells

I had been in Mexico almost two months. It was time to leave my base in the city, and go north. To go, that is, to Hermosillo. From there, after I had explored the region of the Sonoran desert, I planned to travel across the mountains to Chihuahua, by way of Creel; a small town near the Copper Canyon, which some people told me was more spectacular than the Grand. (At which others said 'What? Oh don't be ridiculous!'). And from Chihuahua I planned to go to the industrial city of Monterrey, and from Monterrey to Nuevo Laredo, and the border.

But before I could set off – by train, I had decided – I had to say my goodbyes in Mexico City; and to thank everyone who had put themselves out for me, and allowed themselves to be used by me. And though, while saying my goodbyes, nothing very unusual or exciting happened, I did seem to hear an echo of all the themes I had heard before in the course of my round of friends old and new. Or if not hear an echo, be given – or in one case find myself giving – another line, another little piece of shading or colouring to the portrait I was working on; my picture of Mexico.

There was Eugenia, for example, with whom I was supposed to go out for dinner. But when I went round to her apartment, she told me she couldn't leave the house, because her daughter, who had flown down to Chile the night before, seemed to have disappeared, and she had to wait by the 'phone. Her situation – that of the intelligent, bright, high-toned and attractive exile looking for a lost relation – was typical of a whole section of Mexico City society. It was a section, not necessarily non-Mexican, that paid lip-service to Latin-Americanism, felt that ultimately its roots were in Europe, yet felt, equally, bound to this country. Bound not only by its lip-service, but by the fact that, however mixed its feelings, and however much it would have preferred either to be elsewhere in Latin-America (somewhere brighter, more intelligent, more high-toned and attractive), or away in Europe itself, it had to admit that Mexico had given it both a place in a culture it could, more or less, feel a part of, and, more importantly, freedom. A freedom that, until very recently, would have been denied it in most other countries of Latin-America (and would still have been denied it in some).

Shabby, corrupt and ugly though Eugenia and her like found it – or found its inhabitants – at least here, where the general absence of idealism was tempered by a pragmatic sense of what was or was not necessary to keep a society just about running – by a pragmatic sense of good and evil, rather than by any absolute, god-given sense – they could continue their search for whoever or whatever they had lost, and continue it with a relative sense of security. And if the worst came to the worst and the loss should prove definitive – at least here, under the volcanoes and amidst the flowers, they could mourn their loss in peace.

Then there were the Fs, whose farewell present, whose parting message as it were, was to put on their most elegant clothes – Mr F in a pale impeccable suit, Mrs F in a white crêpe de Chine outfit, with white silk stockings, with strings of pearls round her neck, and a single gold and jade bracelet on her wrist – and to drive me very slowly, as if in a procession, round all the wealthy suburbs I hadn't yet seen. Round, therefore, more quiet tree-lined streets with well-watered and manicured grass verges, behind whose high, almost impregnable and bougainvillaea covered-walls stood, presumably (one could very rarely see them) the villas of the rich.

'Of the very very rich,' Mr F told me sadly. 'Of our movie-stars and industrialists.'

'And of our politicians,' Mrs F laughed.

What was their last gesture to me but a way of saying 'This is the only Mexico we can bear to look at, or want you, as a visitor, to see'? The impenetrable flower-covered façade of Mexico, behind which . . .

But no, we do not wish to know about the 'behind which'. For there – beyond the villas, beneath the villas, above, by the side and all around the villas – lies poverty and misery. Lies ignorance and dirt and disease. Lies the loss that other people you know would mourn. And we – we do not have the strength to gaze on that, especially gaze on it uselessly. So we will love our children and our grandchildren, and we will put on our best clothes, and we will be kind and decent and generous and polite. And we will hope, whatever history may teach us to the contrary, that an individual's personal conduct may, in however infinitesimal a degree, affect that history and the course of the world.

And even if it doesn't – this way, perhaps, we will have a chance of happiness . . .

Georgina took me to a concert, given by the Venezuelan ambassador in the courtyard of Chapultepec Castle. The concert was to celebrate the anniversary of some treaty of friendship that had been signed between Mexico and Venezuela; and was memorable principally because of the speech the ambassador made; and the way in which he made it. He was a mournful, rather weary looking man, with something of the walrus about him; and having climbed onto the conductor's podium, and cleared his throat, he started by welcoming – mournfully, weari- ly, and very, very slowly – every possible variety of person who could have been there – Governors, ministers, senators, fellow- ambassadors, conductors, members of the orchestra, ladies, gentlemen, and I'm not sure who else besides. He went on to give the entire history of both Venezuela and Mexico; concentrating, in the latter case, on its more glorious moments. And he concluded by singing a hymn of praise as it were to the Mexico that had always given refuge to political exiles; and had always set an example in the way of freedom, tolerance, independence and democracy to the other countries of Latin America.

'And there you have the official version of the facts,' Georgina whispered to me as the audience, disturbed by the ambassador's eventual silence, applauded briefly and settled down to what would turn out to be, in the enclosed space of the courtyard, such a deafening account of Wagner's Rienzi overture that at the end of it Georgina and I decided we would prefer a drink, and left.

Yes, I wanted to tell her, that's true. And yet – not so. For one couldn't help feeling that the man's very air of mournful weari- ness, if it hadn't exactly given the lie to everything he was saying, had, somehow, allowed one to hear the other side of the story.

The abuses, the thefts, the lies. The streak of godlessness and the lack of idealism. All the failure, or failures, of love . . .

So that at the end, even if one hadn't been meant to, one had heard the whole thing.

The entire history of Mexico.

To Gerardo – and to Mrs B – my farewell consisted of a speech, made in reply to Mrs B's question 'Well then what do you think of us Mexicans?' that I probably shouldn't have given, and that I warned them in advance would undoubtedly be patronizing and ridiculous. 'Since I don't see how you can answer a question like that without being patronizing and ridiculous.' Nevertheless, I added, I was going to make it anyway.

One always does.

'Well,' I started, sitting in Mrs B's garden, as the old lady pottered around watering her plants, 'I'm not sure what to say. Other than that everyone has been unfailingly kind and generous to me. But if I have to say something, and if I have to generalize, it seems to me that the one over-riding feature of the Mexicans, or of almost every Mexican I have met, is that they are – as compared to a European, at any rate, or an American, or even those other Latin Americans I have met – in a way rather . . . simple. That sounds rude, doesn't it? But I don't mean it in an idiot way. I don't mean simple-minded. It's just that – well – most Mexicans, as they stand in the sun let's say, don't seem to see, or don't want to see, that they are casting a shadow. And by *that* I mean . . .'

By that I meant that most Mexicans seemed to me to be unwilling to take any moral responsibility for their position in the world, or to accept that their actions had any moral consequence. It was as if they wanted their lives, and everything they did, to be entirely isolated, without past, present or future, without cause and, as far as possible, without effect. If you don't look round, their attitude appeared to be, you won't see that your shadow is falling on someone else. And if you don't look round, you won't see that your body is obscuring the sun.

That was not to say that they were 'conscience-less,' or 'immoral', – or no more nor less than anyone else.

Obviously they knew 'how to behave' as well as the next man. And no doubt felt just as guilty as the next man when they did something that they thought wrong. It was just that they didn't seem willing to accept that merely by being alive, merely by being 'Mexican', they were already in a moral, and, one might say, political position; and that whatever they did was not going to alter this fact.

Of course other people didn't go round constantly thinking about their 'moral position', always rubbing their foreheads and worrying about where they were standing. But they were instinctively aware of it; and everything they did, however much they might have denied it, was done in the light of this awareness. For example, I said, as a further generalization, the Europeans on the whole were so appalled by the size and the darkness of their shadows that they were tempted – more and more tempted – to take what one could call the Mexican solution, and pretend that they didn't exist at all. While the Americans, on the whole, though equally aware of their shadows, didn't think them too long or dark at all, but, on the contrary, on the small side, and not in any case worth fretting about. Indeed, in order for the United States to continue to play the part it now did in the world, and for them to continue to occupy the position that they did, they were prepared to put up with shadows a good deal longer. As it was – they were hardly a burden at all, and no more than people should expect to bear for the privilege of being an American. Quite neat and satisfactory. Whereas the Mexicans . . .

'Whereas the Mexicans,' I said, 'try not to see a thing.'

Perhaps it was because the sun was so directly overhead here, I suggested, noting that as we sat or stood in that garden we were truly hardly casting any shadows. Or perhaps, I went on, after Mrs B had simply nodded and said 'Mmmm', and Gerardo had asked me why I thought this was so, it was because in a sense they tended not to look up at the sun – tended not to look into the sky searching for visions. They kept their eyes fixed on the earth the whole time. So they knew the possibilities and the practicalities of the earth. Which, naturally, was fine. Only not looking up and seeing the sun – they couldn't know if they obscured it.

Though maybe, I concluded, that is the best way. Never looking up, never looking back, and never worrying about the shadow that one casts. About which one can't do very much anyway. At least that way one does see the earth in front of one. And at least that way one doesn't risk being dazzled. Or treading on things. Or falling . . .

And my farewell to José and Sonia, my hosts, on my last morning in Mexico City, took the form of what turned out to be a sort of dramatic recreation of at any rate part of the speech I had, however unjustifiably, made to Gerardo and Mrs B the afternoon before. A recreation that began with us going with a friend of theirs, on another of Mexico City's bright, clear, sunny Sunday mornings, to a market some four or five streets away; where they wanted to show me the flowers, and I wanted to buy them some flowers.

We wandered from stall to stall. We looked to see which had the widest selection and what looked like the freshest pickings. And Sonia, as if she were checking on the quality of a chicken, touched and probed and sniffed and felt, to make sure everything was as she wanted it to be, or thought it should be.

And then – then we indulged in a sort of floral orgy.

I bought the flowers that I had wanted to buy for these two former strangers who had put me up, been so hospitable to me, and had insisted that I consider their home my home. (Flowers I didn't, half the time, know the names of, but which were all, in their different ways, bright, scented, and – of course – beautiful.) Then Sonia, though she had already said she didn't have enough vases or pots at home, decided that she wanted to get some too.

'I just like *buying* them,' she said, as she asked the old woman at the stall what those were, and those, and those – and told her she'd just have a few – a small bunch – of each.

But Sonia having bought some – Felipe, their friend, who was spending the day with them, also decided it was his duty, or his pleasure, to buy . . .

Well, just one – or two – roses – and some of those white things there – oh, and just a couple of these . . .

We staggered out of the market into the now very hot morning almost invisible beneath our burdens, and decided we'd better take them home before returning to the market to have some breakfast.

'We look like a carnival float,' José said.

'We look like we robbed a flower shop!'

We went down one street – and I wished I had a photograph of the scene, to remember it by. We went down a second street – and I wished someone I knew would see the scene, so it would be remembered for me. We went down a third street . . .

And there, as we were crossing that third street on our way back to the apartment, we saw ahead of us, walking slowly down the dazzling sidewalk in shorts and a T-shirt, an obviously exhausted young American, laden down with two equally obviously very heavy suitcases. He looked as if he had been up all night, and there was sweat and dust on his face, and on his legs, and on his shoes. But – though it was difficult to imagine where to, since there were no hotels or hostels in the neighbourhood, and he wasn't heading towards the Metro – he was keeping going, his face grim, strained, – but determined.

Until, at any rate, he saw us. And then the sight of all those flowers, being carried by four clean, reasonably cool, and well-pressed people seemed to be too much for him. He stared at us. He shook his head as if to say 'It's all right for some.' He smiled at us in an almost sad, though friendly way, and nodded. And then he sat down on a door step, and rested his head on his knees.

'The idealist, overcome by flowers.'

It was time to leave.

TWENTY

Going North

Though fearful, I am not normally paranoid. However, when one arrives at a station and sees that every carriage except one of an at least twenty carriage train is modern, polished and shiny, and finds that (naturally, one tells oneself) one has been put in the single grimy, old-fashionable car, whose windows are obviously dirty despite the fact that the lights aren't working inside, and whose air-conditioning isn't working either (though one is assured, without much conviction, that it will be 'as soon as we're moving'), then paranoia is likely to surface in even the most balanced of minds.

'Why *me*?' one asks oneself, as one keeps switching the lights on and off, unable to believe that there's not a glimmer from any of them. 'What have I done to deserve this?', as one sees the other passengers strolling past, looking relaxed and cheerful, confident that they are going to spend a pleasant night in their cool, bright cabins. And, once again, 'But why *me*?', as the attendant tells one there's not an empty seat anywhere on the train, and that while sometimes the lights in this car do go on when the train moves, other times they don't. And as tonight he can't find the electrician who knows how these things work, he's afraid that . . . 'Well,' he says, almost indignantly, as if he can't understand why I'm so upset, 'At least your fan's working.'

So it is, as it is in the compartments of everyone else who has had the misfortune to be given a place in this carriage. But that – until, half an hour after we pull out, when an emergency light flickers on in the corridor – is all that is working.

We stand around feeling collectively persecuted and discriminated against.

'But I booked weeks ago,' the woman who has the compartment opposite mine moans. 'I bet half the people who only booked yesterday or this morning have all got perfectly good places.'

'They should give us a discount, at least,' the man next to me complains. 'I don't see why *we* should have to pay the same as *them*.'

'It's typical,' the grandmother who was hauled on board only seconds before we left sighs. 'Typical. Most of those other cars are only going as far as Guadalajara. Just one night. But this is going all the way through to Nogales, and Tijuana. Two days! Two days in this inferno!'

'Yeah, but what do you expect?' the American from down the corridor mutters to me. 'This is Mexico. Things like this always happen in Mexico. At least,' he adds, 'they always happen to me.'

But after a while most of us are silent, just waiting in the darkness, watching the street lamps outside pass slowly by, and wondering how we are going to wash our teeth – and get through the night – without being able to see.

I remember the cockroach in Patty and Enrique's compartment on the train to Oaxaca, and peer into my own potential cockroach nest.

One young woman retires into her black hole and sits staring straight ahead of her, like a nun meditating in her cell . . .

With the emergency light in the corridor things became a little easier. One could at any rate make out enough to be able to pull one's bed down from the wall and check that the sheets didn't have insects running all over them. Nevertheless, as I decided that the only thing to do was go to sleep, and wait till morning gave us some light, I still couldn't help muttering a few more 'Why me?s', and thinking that I had been specially selected by fate for misfortune.

My only consolation was that despite all the time I had spent in Mexico City, no earthquake had managed to get me while I was there. So I had cheated the gods to that extent.

Dawn came early, illuminating the high, bleak but fertile land around Guadalajara. And once I was able to see, my spirits rose considerably. I hadn't been bitten or attacked in the night, the compartment was perfectly clean and pleasant, and I had the prospect of a whole day of travel ahead of me; which I planned to spend reading, doing a little writing maybe, and looking, most of the time, out of my window.

What more could one ask for, I told myself as we pulled into Guadalajara station, and the American from down the corridor told me not to have breakfast there, as it was filthy. 'At least – it was three weeks ago, when I was on my way down.' Moving through a landscape one has never seen before, having nothing to do but relax, confident (for an electrician had been promised as soon as we reached Guadalajara) that tonight, when it gets dark, there will be light – if it isn't quite my idea of heaven, it's certainly not bad.

And not bad, or even better than not bad, the morning and most of the afternoon of that day turned out to be.

The view from the window was, according to my diary, 'mountainous, spectacular, and Byronic.' The restaurant car on the train served good food. (I suggested to the American that he might like to eat with me, but he shook his head. He'd eaten on one of these trains before. And they were terrible. At least – no, on the whole, he'd prefer to stick with his apples and cheese.) The people working in the fields, or riding on their horses and donkeys by the track, all seemed friendly, and waved, making one feel that it was still quite special to travel by train. (Except for one surly horseman who gave the train – or was it, paranoia returning, *me*? – the finger. Even if it hadn't been for me, it unsettled me for a while, and made me reflect upon the fragility of the earth's crust.) And the notes I had taken over the previous weeks, and the sort of diary I had kept, didn't – as I settled down into my seat to read them – seem to me altogether meaningless. On the contrary, though they referred to very recent events, they made me feel almost nostalgic.

On the road to Guanajuato

'The children all hurrying somewhere. But where? There is not only no school along this road. There is nothing. Nothing at all. Just the hills, and the cactus, and the stones – and, very occasionally, sitting by the roadside, a young man, his chin resting on his knees, gazing out over the hills, and the cactus, and the stones.

In fact the only people who seem to be going anywhere in this part of the world are the women. They stand alone by the roadside, or in small groups, with their bright shawls and their bags, waiting for the bus to take them to the nearest market. Or maybe just to take them away from their breeze-block dwellings; away, for even an hour, from the earth, the dogs, their children, their husbands and the cactus. Everywhere, everywhere – the cactus.

'How can they bear it?' one asks oneself as one drives by and sees these women – and their husbands, and their children, and the young men. How can they bear the unrelieved grimness, the never-ending labour that scratching a living out of this earth must entail?

Moreover, one knows that one is not alone in asking oneself this question. One is not just being the tourist.

The faces of both women and men, their way of walking, their way of holding themselves, everything proclaims it. What makes us do it? How can we bear it?

It is also the question they ask God, one imagines, as suddenly, in the middle of this stony, open land, one comes across a vividly clad group of perhaps fifty pilgrims marching off to some shrine, clutching their shiny banners with the image of the Virgin or some saint, on them.

What makes us do it?

How can we bear it?

But God, in such a place, is undoubtedly silent. Or at best tells them: Wait.

Wait, and wait, and wait . . .'

The Bad Samaritan

'On my way to meet Georgina last night I saw an old tramp sprawled across the sidewalk, his head resting against the railings of the Alameda Park. A bottle lay by his side. He was groaning slightly, and some sort of liquid was trickling from him towards the gutter. I took it for urine or spilt wine – though I didn't look too closely – stepped over it, and hurried on towards the corner of the park, some hundred and fifty yards beyond the tramp, where I had my appointment with Georgina.

When I got there, however, she hadn't arrived, and as I waited I stood watching two stocky, fair-haired, tied and jacketed and rather officious youngish Americans remonstrating with a couple of small, dark, and uncomprehending policemen. They had been robbed, I guessed, or were lost.

Suddenly the more vocal of the two Americans – a man in his late twenties or early thirties with a crew cut and a shiny pink indignant face – spotted me watching, and without a moment's hesitation came marching over to me.

"You speak Spanish?" he demanded.

"Err – yes – mm – some –" I hesitated.

"Well come over here and explain to these guys then. There's some old man lying on the sidewalk up there," – he pointed towards the tramp – "and he's injured. There's blood all over the place. We're just trying to make these guys understand. They've got to do something about him. You tell them."

Me? Tell two Mexican policemen their duty? Tell them they've *got* to do something? You must be out of your mind, I wanted to say to my righteous bully. You don't tell policemen in this country what they've got to do. Haven't you seen the films? Haven't you read the books? They'll just laugh if I say anything of the sort. I mean look at them with their military uniforms, their guns, their dark eyes, their sullen hostile expressions. Laugh, or hit me, or arrest me for insolence.

Besides, this city must be full of old tramps lying on the sidewalk. What's so special about this one?

Besides, how do you know it was blood?

Besides, why pick on me . . .

Suspecting that I would get in more trouble with the virtuous if I didn't do as I was told, than I ever would with the wicked if I did – and feeling all at once both sullen and hostile myself, and rather sorry for and understanding of the policemen, who were scarcely more than teenagers – I went over and gave the pair the message.

That is, I smiled, said "Buenos noches", and murmured that these two señores were trying to tell them that there was a wounded man lying just up there – now it was my turn to point – and that perhaps he needed help. There was blood all over the sidewalk . . .

I took a step back, waiting for the inevitable reaction.

"Un hombre herido?" repeated one of the men.

"Si."

They turned; they looked; they saw.

They turned back, they nodded (gravely), and the one who had spoken before said "Muchas gracias."

Then they walked the hundred or so yards to the tramp (we stood, watching), flagged down a passing police-car, and with what, at that distance, looked like great care and gentleness, lifted the old man into the back of the car.

The thought that came to me as I watched the car drive away – Hmm, who knows what they'll do to him as soon as they've turned the corner – did not make me feel any more worthy.

"Thank you," one of the two Americans said as they stepped off the edge of the sidewalk and prepared, with wonderful self-confidence, to negotiate the six lanes of traffiic that lay between them and their hotel. And "Yes, thanks a lot," said the other.

"That's okay," I muttered, as modestly as I could.

For what, I wanted to ask.

"Have a good evening!"

"Thanks," I told them as I saw, coming up out of the subway, Georgina. "And you."

"Friends of yours?" Georgina asked as she approached.

"No," I said, as I saw them reach the other side of the road, and stride purposefully into their lobby. "No," I repeated. "No friends of mine."'

Vera Cruz to Xalapa

'Curious trees. They are absolutely leafless, as if they had died, or it were still midwinter. But here and there on their bare branches there are flowers – large, bright, and very vivid. Yellow. Orange. Red. I have seen these trees all over the country, but here they practically line the roadside.

"What are they called?" I say to Georgina, as, climbing slowly up into the mountains and leaving, much to Georgina's disappointment, the heat behind, we pass yet another cluster of them; whose flowers, this time, are purple.

"I've no idea," says Georgina, and laughs. "I'm really not very good as a guide, am I? I suppose I'm not very good as a Mexican. I don't know much about the past. I don't know much about the Indians. And to cap it all – I don't even know the names of the flowers."'

In Coyoacan

'The balloons, the ice-cream, the spun-sugar sellers, and Tom Jones on the loud speaker.

"Why, why, why, Delilah?"

Yet – Coyoacan's square is big enough to take it; and the mimes, and the acrobats, and the jugglers as well. And somehow, all one gets from the confusion, and the colours, and the music – and aside from Tom Jones there are barrel organs being played on every corner, and violinists standing amidst the box hedges – is an impression of people, rather quietly, enjoying themselves.'

*

And to think, I told myself as I returned my eyes to the window, and saw that we had started our descent towards the Pacific coast, that I hadn't wanted to come here . . .

The train gathered speed.

'Hi,' my American travelling companion said a few minutes later, stopping outside the door of my tiny and, as the sun moved west, increasingly hot cabin. 'How you doing?'

'Fine,' I said. 'And you?'

The man nodded. 'You know that they've had four derailments on this section of the track in the last couple of months? They go too fast, and the lines are old, and – boy, did you feel that?'

I did, and deciding that life was not long enough to hear any more complaints about Mexico, made some excuse and went along to the observation platform at the back of our carriage; to take a better look at the incline we were going down, and to calculate my chances if we did come off the tracks.

But – and after half an hour, and being covered in dust, and getting grit in my eye, I was becoming fairly philosophical about the possibility of our crashing – it was not what I saw as the danger of our situation that spoiled that day; turning a not at all bad morning and early afternoon into an uncomfortable late afternoon and evening. Nor even the gloomy American. It was the heat, and the fact that once we got down to sea-level, and were travelling north along the coast, the sun was shining directly through my unopenable windows. I tried various remedies. I went back to the observation platform; where, along with the dust and the grit, I had to put up not only with my gloomy though quite pleasant American, but with a not at all pleasant American from another carriage, who was an unnerving loud-voiced wild-eyed man and shouted at me that he lived in Mexico in a shack by the sea and was going back to the States for a couple of weeks 'to spread the word'. Having fled from the disturbing messiah, I retreated to the observation platform of the carriage behind ours; and there met two Mexican liquor salesmen who first started talking to me, and then proceeded to invite me back to their wonderfully cold and air-conditioned cabin. Where we all got plastered on brandy and coca-cola, and I got such a headache that I winced as I looked at the photographs of their wives and children, and listened to their complaints about the dirty ugly Mexicans of the south who were, according to them 'all Indians you know; lazy stupid and uncivilized'. And then having thanked the salesmen for their booze, and having told them that I had to go and get on with the writing of my book – assuring them, truthfully, that they would be in it – I went to sit in the crowded, noisy bar, and washed the brandy and coke down with a beer. But eventually I decided that to boil was best – or least worst – and simply sat stunned in my compartment, willing the sun to set, and trying to convince myself that once it had the room would suddenly become cool.

'Why me?' I started up again, in time with the train, as I thought of all those other cars, and how comfortable I would be now if I were in one of them, stretched out with a book, or listening to some music. 'Why me? Why me? Why me?'

All the same, there were compensations. The thought that tomorrow morning I would be getting off this train. The fact that however hot it was I did have this little cabin to myself, and thus could escape messiahs, liquor salesmen and anyone else if I wanted to. And the sight, as night fell, of a single horsemen making his way, very slowly, down the middle of a wide shallow river towards the sea. A wide shallow river that seemed to have absorbed all the remaining light, for it alone glowed silver in the surrounding dark countryside. And a river that must have been pointing due west, for in the very centre of the silver ribbon, just where the horseman was riding, was a thin thread of scarlet, left over from the now set sun.

'Heading home', the picture might have been called . . .

That night my sleep was disturbed not only by the heat, which didn't diminish until three or four in the morning, but also by the fact that no one seemed sure what time we would arrive, or even what time we were due to arrive, in Hermosillo. So I fretted, and woke up every hour, afraid that I was going to miss my stop. I shall probably drop off just before we arrive, I told myself, and sleep right through to midday.

But of course my worrying was unnecessary, and at eight twenty-two the next morning, tired but relieved, I was standing on the platform at Hermosillo, saying goodbye to the liquor salesmen, and making sure I had all my belongings. That's another bridge crossed, I told myself; another hurdle overcome. And now if I can just get through this last stage of my journey . . .

I looked around for Patty.

TWENTY-ONE

Hermosillo

For a few minutes, and for the first time since I had arrived in Mexico, I felt I had been abandoned.

The other passengers who had gotten off had disappeared, welcomed by family, friends, or relatives. The train, which was going on to the border – to safety! – pulled out. The sun, though it was only eight-thirty, was already burning. And all around the dry air, the light, and the low yellow hills in the distance reminded me that this was a desert town, and was not, therefore (I told myself) hospitable to man.

All my dislike of travelling returned. All the sense of well-being I had had on the train, the sense of being on the move, of going somewhere I would be welcome – left me. I was alone in a desert town, and my only comfort was a not too far off highrise topped with a Holiday Inn sign, written red against the blue cloudless sky.

If necessary, I thought, I will take refuge there, and plan my next step from a hotel room.

Obviously my letter to Patty, confirming my arrival, had never reached her. Or she had decided to call the bluff of one whose method of travelling was to throw himself into the arms of friends, and hope they caught him.

She had taken a step back, and I had fallen on my face.

Telling myself not to be ridiculous, I crossed the deserted station hall and went towards a telephone; knowing however that I would find no one at Patty's number. Alone . . .

At which point the tiny conflict in my mind between the sense of my own absurdity and the sense of my own courage in facing the unknown, came to an end. Patty hurried into the station hall and shrugged.

'*You* didn't know what time the train would arrive!' she said. '*They* didn't know what time the train would arrive.'

The night before, when she had 'phoned the station, they had said at six-thirty. When she had got to the station at six-thirty this morning they had looked at her as if she were mad, and told her no one could have said six-thirty. And when she had asked at what time the train from Mexico City *would* then get in, they said – well – er – why didn't she try around eight-forty.

It sounded like a convincing time, so she did.

And here she was – late. 'I am sorry,' she said. 'Did you think you'd been abandoned?'

I smiled, as if to say 'don't be so ridiculous,' and told her 'No, of course not.' Then I paused. 'But before we leave here – let's just look at the timetable. To see what time *that* says the train was due in.'

The timetable consisted of a list of just three trains, written in chalk on a blackboard. And according to this list the Mexico City-Nogales Express was due at Hermosillo at precisely eight-twenty. At precisely eight-twenty it had arrived.

We both smiled, and Patty shook her head.

'The trouble is,' she sighed as we walked to her car, 'even the Mexicans believe in the myth of their own unpunctuality.'

*

'A desert town' has a nice ring about it. 'An island in the middle of a sea of sand'. 'An oasis in the waterless waste'.

In fact, the land round Hermosillo is properly defined as semi-desertic; which means that, unirrigated, it can sustain the growth not only of the occasional cactus, but of mesquite, thorn-trees, and other scrubby plants that are able to withstand great heat. Also, while from the empty platform of a strange station the sight of a Holiday Inn rising from the flat earth might look like a fist of civilization, raised defiantly against the surrounding barbarity, once I was in the car, and we were driving down wide, spotlessly clean and tree-lined avenues, I saw that the hotel, though new, was by no means the lonely isolated gesture I had believed it to be. On the contrary, the whole city seemed to be taking a stand against the waste; and, far from having the air of some outpost in the wilderness, some dry, bleak place where the presumably limited quantities of water didn't prevent the dust from getting not only into one's eyes and mouth, but also, as it were, into one's soul, it looked like a prosperous, pleasant town, with much shade from the overhanging branches of what were known locally as Yucateca trees, ('Yucatecas,' said Patty, 'because they have small bodies and big heads,'), with a sense of general fertility if not exuberance, and with – inevitably – flowers, everywhere. The usual bougainvillaea. African tulips. And others whose names I didn't know, or didn't, as we drove past, have time to look at properly.

One just saw the colours. Violet. Crimson. Turquoise. White . . .

'It's the heat that's the problem here,' Patty said. 'That's the thing that's really hard to bear. I mean this is cool for us today.' (It was already thirty-seven degrees centigrade) 'In the summer it regularly gets up to fifty.'

'Fifty?!'

'Yes. And then you can't do anything. You just have to stay home with the air-conditioning on, if you're lucky. If you're not . . .'

Patty shrugged.

'The heat, and the boredom.'

But she added this second drawback more as a formality, I felt, than as a real complaint. As if while she was bored here she didn't really mind being bored. Or as if she liked her life here in spite of the boredom.

'And so you should,' I would tell her later, when we were discussing the absence of anything to do in Hermosillo. ('Apart from work. Apart from going to the movies. Apart from going to the beach. Apart from sitting around.') 'It's beautiful here.'

'Yes? Not if you have to live here always.'

*

But whether a genuine complaint, or simply a gesture, similar to that of Miguel's grandmother when apologizing for her food, that the province-dweller felt was owed to the city, this faint note of longing for the outside world seemed to me, as I got to know Hermosillo better, to be the leit-motif of the whole place; the sound that the city made when struck by a visiting consciousness. A sound that was accompanied by an only very slightly rueful acknowledgement, on the part of at least some of Hermosillo's inhabitants, that all in all life wasn't so terrible here; and that they were, when you came down to it, fairly happy.

And though in the course of my stay I was to meet various people I had never met before, and see sights I had never seen before, if I had to conjure up just one image that captures the flavour of this northern Mexican town, it would be that of Patty and her younger sister Irma sitting in the shaded living-room of their house, listening to Ana-Sofia, the youngest of the three sisters, playing Debussy and Chopin on an only just-out-of-tune piano.

They were three intelligent, attractive young women, Patty a professor, Irma, the only married one, a teacher of 'difficult' children, and Ana-Sofia a student at the University. They had their work, they had an apparently close family life, and though no doubt they all had problems of one sort or another, they gave the impression that whatever problems they did have they would always be able to overcome them, with the aid of their own intelligence and their family's support. And yet – they listened to that sad music murmuring to them of places they hadn't been to and might never go to; they made one think, inevitably, of those other Three Sisters, all longing to go to Moscow; and the very way they sat, and were regarded by their widowed and almost painfully melancholy mother when she came into the room, cried out – or whispered – that for all their work, their brightness, their attractiveness, their *niceness*, they did wish that somehow, somewhere, something – would happen.

This sprinkling of dissatisfaction, one seemed to hear them add, was what made their contentment bearable. Without it they might have been sickened by it, or even brutalized by it.

As brutalized as the poor of Hermosillo, in their tin-roofed shacks, must have been by the summer sun.

*

We drove round the shanty-towns of Hermosillo, Patty, Irma and I, on my first afternoon in the city. 'So you won't think it's all wide flowering avenues here, and prosperity,' Patty said, as Irma gave me the statistics. She told me how, naturally, most of the children she had to take care of, and teach, came from areas like these. How in some families – in one she knew – every one of nine children was blind; their sight destroyed either by congenital diseases, or by malnutrition. How most of the 'houses' had no running water, and many had no running water near. But just as I had been unwilling to make a special visit to the slums in Mexico City, here too, as we bumped down the rutted roads, avoiding the stones and the dogs and the children, I told myself that in a way to drive through such places, or to stop in such places and talk to the inhabitants, is not as good a way of learning the truth about them as it is to imagine what such places are like; and what living in such places is like.

The eye sees; the nose perhaps smells; the brain records. And one comes away sobered by the knowledge that there are people living in the world in such conditions. As one does by the inescapable feeling that, in however small a degree, to some extent their being there is a result of you, in your air-conditioned car with your plane ticket and your traveller's cheques in your pocket, being here. Nevertheless – one cannot see what it is like to be born and brought up in a place like this, where your being there depends on no choice of your own. One cannot know the effect on not just the nose, but on all the senses, that the continual presence of decomposing and rotten matter must have; particularly if there is no escape from it. And one cannot record with one's brain what must be the most unbearable of all aspects of life in the lower depths. The knowledge that if one really, really worked, sweated, suffered – and was very lucky – one might be able to get away; combined with the knowledge – which must be the knowledge of the great majority of the population of the slums in Mexico or anywhere else – that one is too weak, too sick, too depressed, or too, in any case, debilitated, to make that effort to leave. And so, one realizes, one is condemning oneself, and one's children, to yet more brutality, and to being further, to being endlessly, brutalized.

One cannot see, one cannot smell, one cannot record – but one can imagine. Imagine, whoever one is, under whatever circumstances one lives. Imagine the heat, imagine the stench, imagine the wretchedness of it all. For there are no limits to the imagination. Just as, one suspects, there are no limits to the wretchedness. And so, if one will – one can set off. One will probably get far nearer the truth than one ever would if one went there in person. And one will certainly get far nearer than if one went on a guided tour; in a so-called 'true' book . . .

*

If some matters are not, in my opinion, fit subjects for guided tours, others, I hope, are. Therefore, as Irma's husband Alfonso said to me one afternoon, soon after my arrival: 'How would you like to go into the desert, and visit a behaviourist commune?'

Alfonso was tall, pale and ginger-haired, a child psychologist and a composer, who was afflicted with the same strain of melancholy as everyone else in Hermosillo, and sat around much of the time either playing very quietly to himself on a guitar, or working his way through Bach's 48 Preludes and Fugues on a piano. And to begin with I wasn't certain if I had understood his proposal.

'A what?' I said. 'A commune?' I curled my lip.

'Yes,' Alfonso said. 'You've heard of B. F. Skinner? Who thinks that human behaviour can be scientifically modified, and that people can live in a better way, let's say? And that if we all did the world would be a better place?'

'Yes, I've heard of him,' I said. 'And most of what I've heard I don't like. But if you think they might be interesting – sure – let's go. I mean – they're not a lot of Charles Mansons are they?'

'Oh no,' Alfonso reassured me. 'They're all very pleasant and serious. I've had dealings with them in the past about the children, and – yes, I think you might find them interesting.' He paused. 'You can go with Irma and Patty.'

'You're not coming?'

'No,' Alfonso murmured. 'I've – let's say I don't want to see them at the moment.'

That, of course, made me wonder. Maybe they are a gang of crazies I thought; out in the desert. And who were 'the children' Alfonso had had dealings with them about?

Still, I guessed that if he was prepared to see his wife and sister-in-law go out to the place it couldn't be that bad. And who knows – I might actually find myself attracted to community life. After all, my prejudice against it was not based on any experience. And my aversion to Skinner was not the result of having read any of his books, but simply from having found him personally disagreeable when I had seen him on television; and, so far as I understood them or he explained them properly, his ideas to be both wrong-headed and potentially dangerous.

Maybe, after this morning, I would disappear into the modern equivalent of the monastery, and never be seen again.

I could imagine worse fates . . .

The road out of town took us first past the university where

Patty taught; a university which, being in the very centre of Hermosillo, and being vast, dominated the city, and in fact caused every road out of town and most of the roads in town to go past it. After the university I had a large modern auditorium pointed out to me where, Patty said, Hermosillo's cultural life was conducted. 'A concert every now and then. Sometimes a dance company. But nothing else. Nothing really to make you want to stay here.' After the auditorium we went by a large modern hotel which was also the local brothel. 'Better attended than the cultural centre.' And then – after a left turn, and a right, and a right fork – we were in the desert.

It wasn't until then, as we started the fifty mile drive towards the foothills of the mountains, along a generally straight and always empty road, where the only sign of life was an occasional cow, that I realized how merely semi-desertic this particular part of Sonora was. (The first time I did see a cow I thought 'My God, it's lost out here'. Then I noticed there were others; and that in fact the wilderness was wired off from the road. And eventually the presence of dirt tracks leading away apparently into nowhere, with generally broken down signs constructed roughly over them, made me aware that what I was assuming was nothing was, instead, a ranch.) For not only was there sufficient vegetation to maintain a certain quantity of cattle, but all the mesquite trees we passed – and most of the trees we passed were mesquite – were in flower. So that instead of looking out over a sea of yellow sand – the proper text-book view of any desert – I was looking out over a sea of yellow blossoms.

An ocean of yellow blossoms.

Though Patty and Irma assured me that this was just a one-off affair; laid on by someone who had the interests of my book at heart . . .

'Well thank you,' I told the sisters, 'and it would be nice if someone did organize things like this. But I assume you get a spring here every year, and that, therefore, the mesquite flowers every year.

'Yes of course,' Patty said. 'But never like this. It's because of all the rain we had last year, and the floods. Normally they're in flower just for a couple of days. Then they're all burnt and brown again. But this year – honestly, I've never seen it like this. Ever. And just when you're here.'

'In that case,' I said, 'I will take the responsibility for it. And thank you again. Though I do wish it were always that easy.'

'Flowers in the desert: the Mexican reality.' Illustration please . . .

We were joking, of course, and knew we were talking nonsense.

All the same, looking out of the car window at that great yellow sea, just in a tiny corner of my mind, in the very back of my brain, I thought that maybe, possibly, in a certain sense . . .

No, stop it, I told myself. That way madness lies.

When one starts confusing luck, with magic.

*

The question as to what would happen if one broke down on this road, soon, however, began to replace any idea of magic as the principal subject of my thoughts. That, and the doubt as to whether we were on the right road at all. We hadn't passed anyone. No one had passed us. Apart from those battered ranch entrances we hadn't seen a single house or any indication that there might be one near. And not only had there not been any signposts on the road, but Irma wasn't absolutely convinced that Alfonso, when giving her directions, had said we should fork right leaving town after turning left, rather than fork left after turning right.

Would anyone come along and help us, I wondered; as Patty said 'We *must* be on the right road', and leaned forward in the driving seat as the thought struck her that we might not be. Should we all stay with the car and hope someone does come by?; as Irma, in the back seat, frowned and said 'I'm sure he *did* say fork right.' And – or should we get out and walk, and hope that those ranches do exist – and are inhabited, and will offer help?; as Irma added, putting on her dark glasses, 'If we *are* right, we should come to a village, eventually.'

Yes, but by then we might already have broken down; or we might have too little gas to get back onto any other road, let alone the right one.

Needless to say, we did not break down, and we did eventually come to a village. ('There were gold mines here once. These people must have come, and stayed. But I don't know what they do now.'). Where we were assured that we were heading in the right direction. And after what had, in reality, been little more than an hour's drive in all, we turned off the road, bumped up a long earth track, and arrived at what, if some divine and benevolent editor had laid on the mesquite in the desert to illustrate my contention that Mexico was the land of flowers (and not art or dreams or ideals), that same editor might have laid on to illustrate what art and dreams and ideals might have made of the place.

Los Horcones, as the community was called, up on its hill-top above the Sonoran Desert, had something of the unreal about it.

Not because the land that surrounded it and clearly belonged to it was infertile. Far from it. But because the first person we encountered, when we stopped at what turned out to be a school-house to ask if it was all right if we visited the community, was an almost white-blonde young man with pale blue eyes who, though he spoke to us in Spanish, was clearly not Mexican. Because the seven or eight children who the young man was teaching were all, in some cases severely and very visibly, retarded. And because – precisely because – the land that we drove through, and then, after the track came to an end and we had parked the car, walked through, was so very *not* infertile. It was as if we had stumbled upon the garden of the Eden. There were lemons – nature having made a mistake in solving the anagram? – the size of melons. Corn grew as thickly and healthily as ever corn grew on a farm in the Mid-West. And, wherever one looked or listened, there was water. There was water spraying the crops, and the vegetables, and the trees. There was water flowing down irrigation channels. There was water in a large pond, where ducks and geese splashed about. And a little further up the hill, nearer the community houses, there was water in a large round swimming pool in which a number of other children, and these obviously not retarded, were splashing about, shouting, playing, and laughing.

Seeing this scene, and being soothed by the sense of unreality, my hostility took a step back, and, as it were, sat down.

It did not, however, leave the room; and, when we approached the main house, where two or three Indians were sitting on the long porch in front of it, it was already starting to get to its feet again. These men taking a rest were, I guessed, labourers; and what were labourers doing in a commune, I wanted to know. I thought everyone did his or her share of the work, and shared the fruits of their labour. I did not realize that even here there was a class system, and that paradise had been created by some for the benefit of a few; a few mainly middle-class semi-intellectuals of European descent who could not or would not cope with the outside world, I suspected. Explain, my hostility wanted to say, as a thin denimed man in his mid-thirties came out onto the deck and welcomed us. And – raising an invisible hand – please, I want to know something.

But, naturally, I didn't say any of these things, and having shaken hands with the man, and heard Irma explain that she was Alfonso's wife and had been up here a couple of years ago ('Oh yes, I remember, how are you?'), I accepted the offer of a rocking chair, and prepared, on the whole, to listen.

And after five minutes both my hostility and I were feeling quite comfortable. Our host, who was the appointed spokesman of the community, was quietly-spoken, unassuming and un-dogmatic, and agreed that there were contradictions in the set-up. (Such as the electricity that came in from outside through cables stretching across the desert below and built – this at my sniffiest – 'by other people.') The explanation that he gave as to the aims of the community was almost wry in tone, and certainly not de-livered as a sermon. (What we're doing up here is making an experiment, he insisted, to see whether a different mode of existence is viable. But it was no more than an experiment, he went on, albeit one that had lasted for eleven years now. And one shouldn't think of them as drop-outs, or evaders of social re-sponsibility. Far from it. They were in the forefront of the battle for a better life, a better world, and they certainly weren't people who rejected the modern world. On the contrary, they were in favour of using science and technology of the most advanced kinds to further their aims. Which were, as the information sheet he gave me put it, 'to establish and maintain a society based on CO-OPERATION as an alternative to competition; on SHARING [communal property] as an alternative to individual property; on PACIFICISM as an alternative to aggression; and on EQUALITY as an alternative to discrimination [social differences]'). And while neither he nor the other members of the community – whom one could tell at a glance; they all had fair skin, and half of them fair hair – seemed unnaturally friendly or aggressive, or any more or less happy than Patty, Irma or I, their children, running up and down from 'the children's house' to the large tank that was their swimming pool ('that in turn feeds the duck pond, that in turn is used for irrigation') did seem just as happy as children should be.

So if they're content, I argued, and don't go round wearing the sort of crazy smile one associates with people who feel themselves cut off from nature by birth, and want to live more closely in contact with it than the average person, why should I feel suspicious of them, or sceptical of their way of life?

Why indeed, I murmured to myself, as I rocked back and forth, as bird song and children's voices filled my ears, and I smelled the smell of growth, and ripeness . . .

Because, snarled my hostility, getting bored after its rest, you want to know where the money came from that bought this land. Was it 'alternative' money?

No, said Francisco, when I put this to him. The three original members of the community had put up the cash to buy first some land just outside Hermosillo, and then, after seven years, when the city began to approach them, this place up here.

(Ha. So you need some capital to find an alternative to the capitalist system.)

Well then, my hostility went on – because you want to know what these Indian labourers are doing here. (And, while we're on the subject, why there are no Indians *in* the community.)

'Unfortunately,' was the explanation for this, 'we're still forced to use people from outside to do some of the heavy work – until we have enough money to buy our own bulldozers and trucks. Obviously we pay them the going rate, but – yes, I agree, there's an element of contradiction in that, too.'

(As to the second question – it was hardly worth asking, the answer seemed so obvious. The Indians had only just been, if even now they were, admitted into society as it was. There must have been very few of them who felt themselves already too cut off from nature, too European for this society, and were already seeking an alternative to it. They lacked both the spiritual and physical capital to make the move. Besides, it is hard enough to believe in a flawed, defective dream, let alone in a dream within a dream, however green and prosperous and fertile – and built by your relatives' hands – that latter dream may be.)

And the last reason why you can't just sit back and relax, my hostility informed me, after I had glanced through the pamphlet I'd been given, is because for all this talk of community life, and for all this air of adults – seven men, five women, six children – living together in harmony with each other and the world about them, there's a faint whiff of totalitarianism hanging over this place.

(A whiff that was not dispelled by my being told that nothing was done here without the consent of all the members of the community. It was increased by my reading that 'we have two or three planners, who name the managers, supervise them, replace them and have the responsibility of making decisions for the entire community, taking into consideration the opinion of every member of the community'. And it was turned into something stronger by my observation that there were two men here, our spokesman and one other, who, whatever they might say to the contrary, and however much they might dislike it, were both seen as and saw themselves as 'leaders'.)

And you want to know one final thing.

What if a member contravenes one of the rules of the community? Say, for example – as I saw from the pamphlet was strictly forbidden – a member of the community took drugs. What did they do to that member?

'We expel him or her,' I was told. 'He or she has to leave the community.'

Which was all very well, I reflected. Only – a society cannot 'expel' people it doesn't like, or who won't obey its rules. It can 'punish' them if it likes, and put them in prison. Or it can attempt to 're-educate' them, and make them see the error of their ways. But not, but never, expel them. Not, that is, unless there is some surrounding, inferior community, into which the offending member can be cast out. (Out of the lush green dream, into the one full of holes you can fall through.) But otherwise – no. In one way or another – it has to live with them.

You should distrust the very concept of a superior society, my hostility concluded. And when that superior society can only grow in the middle of that inferior one, and is, ultimately, dependent on it, you should not only distrust it but condemn it utterly.

Yet despite all these reservations I had, and despite the spoken or unspoken protests I made, I couldn't quite bring myself to condemn or reject Los Horcones utterly. It was possible that my perceptions were mistaken, that the explanations given me were neither complete nor entirely understood, and that in any case I was so determined to object to the place that not even proof that this *was* paradise would have been sufficient to overcome my prejudices. Moreover – and again and again it struck me, particularly when we got up from our chairs, and started a tour of the property – these hundred hectares, flourishing up above the Sonoran Desert, were, whatever one said about their origins, beautiful. Ideally beautiful . . .

And probably, had we not, at the very end of our tour, come back to the school-house and the 'behaviourly-deficient' children we had seen on our arrival, and had we not come back to the subject of money, I would have left the place saying 'Yes, well, it's not for me of course', but thinking that despite my protests I might actually have liked it there, or wished I could have lived amidst that beauty. In peace . . .

But come back to both we did, and coming back to them, I found an objection that no amount of peace, or beauty, or suspicion of my own lack of comprehension could outweigh. And it was that these children – these fair, (yes, they too) damaged children – were in very large part the foundation upon which the community rested. While sitting on the deck at the beginning, I had understood our guide to say that they took care of these children up here to show that the damaged could live with the healthy, and live, to a certain extent – unlike the rule-breakers – *within* the community. But when we visited the school-house, were introduced to the children, and I asked how they were paid for, I discovered that far from this being true – or far from it being exclusively true – these children were in fact here to maintain the healthy and the rest of the community.

Their parents – their fair, wealthy parents – paid Los Horcones and its members (Paid them a lot, Patty murmured to me in English; paid them what they could, said Francisco in Spanish) to take care of their off-spring . . .

Take care of them well – very, very well maybe. (For I should say that the children obviously adored all their guardians, with whom they mixed freely, and, in every respect except the obvious one seemed as healthy and happy as the members' own children). But take care of them *out there*, away from us, away from the world. Others may find nothing unusual in this – and certainly the members themselves made no secret of the fact; their leaflet listing 'the education of children with behavioural deficits [sic]' as their first source of financial support. But somehow, for me, the idea that this 'alternative society', this dream within a dream, this whole wonderful experiment in co-operation, sharing, pacificism and equality, was based on the ability of the wealthy to banish their children into the desert was, though perhaps apt, also a little sad, more than a little grotesque, and certainly – even if I felt this instinctively rather than rationally – unacceptable.

A society of the spiritually disabled, paid for by the physically disabled.

No, it wouldn't do.

*

When we left Los Horcones an old Indian who had been working on the land asked us if we would give him a ride back into town. As we did, Irma asked me what I thought of the place, and whether I would like to live there. At which I started off on my 'yes well while it wasn't as bad as I feared and was in many respects very admirable . . .' speech. Also, I said, there are one or two things I can't accept. Take for example – I hesitated – Mario, the ultimate head of the community, though he wouldn't accept the title. Nice, unpompous, unpretentious, but . . .

Mario is a very good man, the old Indian interrupted. I know his father, and I know him. And they are both – very good men.

I took note, and said not another word.

*

Brief visions.

The vineyards stretching mile after mile out into the desert.

The experimental farm where Patty assists in the research into acid soil; that is, in its clinical and less romantic way, as fertile as Los Horcones. Now this, I think, as I look out over the fields of double or triple yield barley and wheat, this, down here on the plains, is the right kind of experiment; not that, up there, *out of this world*.

The absolutely straight road to the sea, the surface covered with small grey birds. Patty drives fast, and I am constantly prepared for slaughter. But at the very last moment, as if playing a game of dare, or testing their own bravery, the birds fly up and off, and avoid us. And though one thinks that occasionally they must misjudge their timing, on the whole hundred or so kilometres to the sea, we don't see a single corpse.

The beach itself; Hermosillo's resort town Kino. Just a single row of mostly closed white houses facing the shore. And a trailer park, where mostly middle-aged to elderly Americans are pottering about, as if disorientated by the lack of anything to do except bathe.

But they do not bathe. For when Patty, one of her colleagues from the research farm, and I go onto the beach, there is not another person on the whole of the immense white stretch of sand. Just the sea, the birds, the island out in the bay, and Patty's voice, as she and Gregorio sit fully dressed by my side, both with their arms around their knees.

'My great-grandparents came over to Mexico from Spain. They had a ranch out in the desert. The Seri Indians who live round here hated the whites. One day they attacked the ranch and burned it down. Everyone was murdered except my grand-mother. She was a small child then, and hid in a laundry basket.'

I do undress and swim, but only for a short time. Because the water is cold and not very clear. Because there is sand in the wind that stings the skin. And because for some reason – Patty's story? the landscape? – the loneliness is oppressive.

Agreeing that we will go to lunch instead, we make our way back to the car. And walking up the beach, and seeing the closed shuttered houses overlooking it, and the trailers and the campers in their parks, though one doesn't know how they pass the day, one feels one understands why those Americans don't bathe.

To get to the restaurant we drive several kilometres along a track through the sand, parallel to the shore. Here there are only cacti; and a little black gathering of vultures. They sit on the ground in a circle, having, it appears, a meeting.

'Are you sure there's a restaurant at the end of this?' I ask, thinking now that the loneliness of the beach was preferable to this desolation.

'Yes, don't worry,' Patty assures me, and turns the wheel sharply to avoid a ditch.

'But what kind of restaurant is it?' I continue as Patty swings the wheel back.

'A good one,' she assures me. 'You'll like it.'

Is this some kind of joke?

Eventually we come to the end of the track and to a largish shack, built on the end of a sand-bar sticking out into an estuary. There is an ancient trailer parked on the lot outside the shack, and a man, sitting on a broken-down jetty, fishing.

Romantic abandon can go no further.

Once inside the shack however everything was different. For a start the decor was 1950's night-club by-the-sea-style, all fishnets and broken mirrors and shark jaws and crab shells and photographs of pop singers and movie stars, hanging from the ceiling, or stuck onto the blue distempered walls. That cheered me up immediately. (As did the fact that we were, of course, the only customers – that they had had in a year, perhaps.) Then the food – the fish – when it came was both fresh, and well-cooked, and the wine they gave us was cold. And finally, though in other circumstances it might have been depressing, the view from the windows out over the estuary or creek – a view of empty water, and of the spars of wrecks; on every one of which sat large grey pelicans that periodically flopped off and flapped away as if overcome with tedium – was so mournful, so much a caricature of a world permanently out of season, that it made us feel quite merry. It made us feel that in the final analysis, a world out of season, an abandoned tacky world with a few old sequins stuck here and there, was, in terms of ease, and comfort, and beauty of the sadder kind, the best of all possible worlds.

Or anyway – as we swatted the flies, as we noted the old tin cans and cast-off tyres lying in the shallow water, and as, on the spar nearest to us, a pelican half lifted its wings and then merely yawned – a world in which one could feel at home . . .

*

I spent a week in Sonora, travelling round, taking notes, meeting people. (The colleagues, the friends, and, in their shaded houses, the relatives. The relatives who welcomed me, offered me drinks, and said they hoped I was enjoying myself in Hermosillo; and the relatives in every one of whose houses someone was playing the piano. Mozart. Schubert. Ravel. Calls, as it were, across the sea.) And I might have stayed longer had I known in advance that when we went, at the end of that week, to a travel agency, to pick up our train tickets to Creel (where we were planning on staying a couple of days before Patty returned to Hermosillo and I continued on to Chihuahua) the girl at the agency would tell us that the rail-link to Creel was suspended because of snow. Even if it were opened, she said, she didn't advise our going as it was below freezing in the mountains, and the only good – the only heated – hotel was fully booked. If I wanted to go to Chihuahua, she added, I would have to fly. As it was, this news threw me off balance, and I lost what little desire I'd had to go to Chihuahua in the first place. So when I 'phoned a cousin of mine in Tucson Arizona whom I hadn't seen in twenty years, and he suggested that I catch a bus up to Nogales the following day – where, if I liked, he would pick me up – I wasn't certain what to say but, delighted at the prospect of once again being met and having friendly arms to fall into, ended up by saying yes, thank you, that would be wonderful.

As I continued to think it would be, even when I discovered I had to get up at five-thirty to catch the bus to the border, and even when it sank in that in this way, and quite unexpectedly, my visit to Mexico was over.

'I feel lost,' I told Patty, when I put the 'phone down. 'One moment I'm expecting to be in Mexico another two or three weeks – and next – I'm off. I am sorry – and I really would have stayed longer if I had known. But . . .'

But an offer of safety is not to be sneezed at.

'I'm sorry too,' said Patty. 'I've got a feeling I'll never get to see Creel now. Though maybe next time you come. Anyway, at least you've seen the north-west.' She looked at her watch. 'And there is one other thing you've got time to see before you go.' She smiled. 'As long as you don't mind getting your clothes dirty, and you're wearing your glasses.'

'I always wear my glasses,' I told her. 'And of course I don't mind about my clothes.' But what was it she wanted to show me, I asked, and why did I not have to mind.

'I'll tell you,' Patty said, looking at her watch again 'or rather you'll see – at a quarter to six. In the meantime – let's go and say goodbye to the family, and see if Irma wants to come.'

*

At ten minutes to six, Patty, Irma and I, having parked the car in front of the cathedral, sat down on a bench in the square opposite; a not very large square, with a bandstand in the middle and a number of Yucateca trees dotted around it in a formal pattern.

'Right,' I asked the sisters. 'And now?'

'You wait,' said the one; and 'be patient' said the other. 'And make sure you keep your glasses on. And keep looking up at the sky.'

'Yes,' I said, 'well?' doing as I was told and seeing nothing but the blue that was now softening as the sun prepared to set; and a number of birds flying into the broad overhanging trees, to roost.

'Be patient, be patient,' the sisters repeated; as I noticed that the 'number of birds' was starting to be a large number, and a number that was increasing all the time.

'In another five minutes . . .'

In another five minutes the birds started to arrive in earnest. And then, for the next hour, as the light slowly faded and the blue became pink and then pearl and then green, there took place the greatest invasion of any one spot by any one species that I have ever seen. Wave, after wave, after wave, until every branch of every tree was heavy, and screaming with them. And that was only the beginning. At twenty second, at thirty second, at minute intervals they came in; great sky-darkening swarms. Those that were already on the trees made room for those that had just arrived, squawked and flapped and found themselves a place, before they had to shift for the next batch. Hundreds of birds. Thousands of birds. Tens of thousands of birds. Maybe even hundreds of thousands of birds. On, and on, and on, until one thought no, that must be all, there can't be any more room. There can't be a twig left to rest on; there can't be a leaf. And as soon as one had told oneself this another wave arrived. And then another. And then another. 'But it's not . . .' and another, and another, and another. 'That *must* be all.' And another, and another. 'I don't believe it.' And another, and another, and another.

The spectacle was extraordinary for a number of reasons. For the sheer quantity of birds. For the noise that they made. (It was so loud I could hear only half the story told by a tough, scarred ten year old who cycled up to us, and started giving us, unasked, an explanation of the birds' behaviour. He went on, when he was asked, to tell us his age and name, that he lived under the bandstand, and that he had run away from his home in Nogales a year ago because his father had been murdered by the man who had gone on to marry his mother, and that this step-father had tended to beat him.) Then – for the way the thickly leaved Yucatecas eventually disappeared and became, apparently, bird trees. For the fact that all the birds that arrived in the square were essentially black in plumage. (All the white feathered birds – ducks? geese? swans?; it was impossible to make out – passed by, high above, on their way to some other destination; immense slowly moving Vs, luminous in the darkening desert sky.) And fifth – for the fact that while there were crows and starlings amongst the crowd, perhaps eighty per cent of the birds were of the same kind.

'Where do they come from, that's what I don't understand,' I said to the sisters, and the sisters put to the urchin; who shrugged, defiantly. 'I mean there's desert all around, and you don't see them in the day in the city. So where?'

But what was most extraordinary about the spectacle was that while the birds that made up the dominant eighty per cent were black-feathered like the crows and the starlings, they were not entirely black-feathered. They had bright orange yellow discs on their breasts. So that as one sat there, looking up as still more, and still more, and still more arrived, the bird trees, the huge invisible Yucatecas, were not just black, but black and orange-yellow. As if, one thought, as the sky now began to lose its colour altogether, these birds, like creatures from a fable, had flown off with the sun, and had brought it here for the night. ('Why the Darkness Falls.') Or as if these trees, in the space of an hour, had magnificently burst into flower.

Into flower, and song.

It was a good way to spend a final evening in Mexico.

*

Next morning, at five, Patty drove me to the bus-station, and gave me a farewell present from her mother – a local speciality made out of the oranges that grow on the trees that line half the streets of Hermosillo. (Or maybe that was what the birds were trying to do. Change the Yucatecas into orange trees.)

At five-thirty exactly, having thanked Patty for her kindness – and having thought that if Mexico were a dangerous place, then Patty and her sisters seemed to demonstrate how best that danger could be overcome; for they gave the impression of loving not merely the appearance of flower, but the flower itself – I got on the bus, and the bus pulled out.

And at a quarter to ten, having finished my final journey in Mexico, and trying in my head to write a final paean to the country I was leaving, I arrived in Nogales.

'This dangerous, lovely land, flawed by the failures of love. This dangerous lovely land, to which disappointment and greed, hunger and curiosity can lead one. This dangerous lovely land which, if travel is a form of self-discovery, is that part of oneself that, finding no consolation in gods or dreams, turns, for forgetting or salvation, to flowers.

This dangerous, lovely land . . .'

But as I was trying to write this, and trying to cope, at the same time, with two bags and a leaking jar of bitter oranges in syrup, I had approached a small beige office. There a dark-haired woman in uniform asked for my passport, asked what I had been doing in Mexico, and when I said trying to write a book, laughed, said Good Heavens, and waved me on through. And thus, without any of the trouble that I had anticipated I would find at the border – without long lines of people, without careful checks into my identity, without a thorough search of my person and my bags, and, which struck me at the time as being less important than my trouble free exit and entrance though afterwards I regretted, without so much as a nod of goodbye to the very place I was attempting to write my paean to – I left Mexico. Left Mexico, arrived in the United States, and, having sat for an hour on a bench in a small garden waiting for my cousin, looking back through the fence that divided the two countries, told myself that whatever came of this trip I had just completed, I had at least survived it.

The sun was shining. People were wandering back and forth across the border in their shorts and T-shirts to go to a Safeway supermarket on this side, or to go to a bullfight on that side. And I – I was on my way home.

It was just another Sunday morning.

TWENTY-TWO

Safety

At which point I should perhaps stop. End of Mexico – end of book. And I would – were it not for three or four things that happened to me, first in Arizona and then, when I flew on to Austin – ostensibly to do some reading at the University library but in fact to see a friend – in Texas. Three or four things which seemed to me to make comments upon all I had observed or done over the past few months.

I say three or four because I am not certain if the sensation I had, in the days after my arrival in the States, that crossing the border had been like passing from the flesh to the spirit, should be included in this list. It may have been too subjective a feeling . . .

The first definite thing that happened was that after my cousin and his wife had picked me up – and thus removed my last source of anxiety – I noticed that while in Mexico the Sonoran Desert had been blooming, here in Arizona, though we were still in the Sonoran Desert, there wasn't a flower to be seen. Anywhere. And not only on the road. For when we reached Tucson, and I looked about me, I realized that while the buildings were modern and clean, and the streets wide and straight, in the city too there wasn't a flower in sight. Trees, yes. Shrubs, yes. Bushes, and grass, and cacti . . .

But the bougainvillaea, but the African tulips, but the other nameless things, all purple and orange and red – where were they?

'Oh,' my cousin smiled, when I put this question to him: 'We're into desert vegetation here.'

By which he meant, I interpreted, 'Here, surrounded by desert, we try to idealize the desert, and thus make it bearable. Whereas there, surrounded by desert, they try with their flowers to forget the desert. And *thus* make it bearable.'

Or, as we turned into his own flowerless street, and pulled up in front of his own flowerless house: 'Here, in the spirit, we feel safer.'

The second thing that made me think I was hearing some sort of comment on my stay 'down south', happened when, after a few days in Tucson spent eating, drinking and talking, I did fly on to Austin. I had thought that my principal motive for going there was to see a friend, and that the chance of using the University library was only a secondary consideration. But once I was there and had started reading – reading, to begin with, to fill in the gaps between meals, walks, and visits to the cinema to catch up on all the films I'd missed while I'd been away – I discovered a book that could have been written just for me.

It was about the Aztecs and their culture; and its principal thesis was that the Aztecs, the last link in a cultural chain that stretched back to the Olmecs, were obsessed with the ephemeral nature of human existence, and despite all the sacrifices they made to their gods, were never wholly convinced or consoled by those gods. Life, not being anchored or given any firm basis by gods, seemed to them like a dream; and their great concern in life was to find a raft of reality to which they could cling.

Where did they look for this raft?

Principally, the author concluded, the literate looked for it in poetry. In the writing – and possibly reading – of poems.

However, there wasn't a precise word for poetry in Nahautl. Instead the Aztecs, when they wanted to say 'poetry', had to use an expression.

Flower and song.

*

'What am I to go with?
those flowers
which have closed?
Will my name be nothing some time?
Will I leave no thing behind me in the world?

At least flowers, at least songs!
How is my heart to work?

Perhaps we come, in vain, to live,
to come like springs upon dry earth.'

*

Clearly, however, flower and song didn't mean only poetry, but also flower, and song. And undoubtedly this consolation of the literate was only an expression of a general feeling, of what the unlettered felt too. So that if the poets – who were generally priests or princes, in any case members of the ruling caste – found consolation, found reality, in flowers and songs as poetry, the average Aztec found consolation, found reality, in the things themselves. In flowers, and songs.

The Spanish destroyed the Aztecs. But that much of their culture survived.

To soothe, and torment, their destroyers.

*

And so to my final stop: in a small air-conditioned office in a house in a back street in Austin.

I had gone to say goodbye to a couple I had met earlier in the week; since the following day I was leaving for Houston, and London. But having said goodbye to the wife, I found I would have to wait half an hour before saying goodbye to the husband; who was tied up for the moment, on business.

Why didn't I, it was suggested, go to meet O in the meantime; who rented a room across the hall to work in. I could talk to her for a while.

O was a writer, too.

The door of the room across the hall having been duly knocked upon and opened, my presence explained, and my apologies given and accepted, I was shown in and offered a chair.

O was a handsome middle-aged woman in a black turtle-neck sweater and grey trousers, who had a voice that was so soft, and an accent that was so southern, that I had difficulty, to begin with, in understanding her. But after a minute or two, and after we had exchanged pleasantries ('I know it's a silly question, but what kind of books do you write?' 'I know I should know this, but have you ever been published here in the States?') I adjusted to her pitch and way of speaking, and she no doubt adjusted to mine, and we settled down to talk of movies, Mexico, ('Oh I just love Mexico. I wish I could spend more time there. We had two wets working for us once.'), and the books we were both working on. Or, in my case, about to be working on.

'It's going to be called "A Dangerous Place",' I said.

And told O how I thought that if Mexico wasn't the physically dangerous place I had been led to believe it was, it did neverthe-less present certain dangers to the European going there; and, I supposed, to the Indians who were already there.

'And I've discovered a book in the library here that sort of backs me up.'

I told her about the Aztecs, and the author's idea that they sought reality in flower and song; in, that is, poetry.

Oh, how interesting, O said, and went on to wonder what 'We Americans' sought reality in now.

Movies, I suggested, above all. Though also theatre, and dance, 'and novels of course'.

But definitely *not* flowers.

Just then the 'phone rang, and O, in mid-sentence, went to answer it.

For almost a minute, after her initial 'Hello', she didn't say a word; simply listening looking faintly pained. Then she put her hand over the mouthpiece and whispered to me 'Salesman'. But she went on listening for another thirty seconds before she finally interrupted her caller.

In fact, when I heard what she said my first reaction was 'How absurd'. Particularly as she didn't appear to be speaking ironi-cally, or to be referring in any way to our conversation. But afterwards, thinking about her reply, it made me laugh, and made me think that here, in this room, I had really come to the end of my Mexican journey.

I had, at any rate, been given the last words for my book on Mexico; and heard a sort of answer to my first.

'Young man,' drawled O, in her softest, most Southern voice. 'Thank you. But I am a writer of fiction, and I do not need insurance.'